WAR IN THE PACIFIC

The most important, explosive, and strategic battles of World War Two took place in the Pacific arena as the seemingly invincible Japanese sought to expand their notorious empire. Now this astonishing era comes to life in a breathtakingly authentic new series by noted historian Edwin P. Hoyt that places the reader in the heart of the earth-shattering conflict—a dramatic, detailed chronicle of military brilliance and extraordinary human courage on the bloody battlefields of land and sea.

VOLUME IX
IWO JIMA

*Other Avon Histories of World War II
by Edwin P. Hoyt*

WAR IN THE PACIFIC
TRIUMPH OF JAPAN
STIRRINGS
SOUTH PACIFIC
ALEUTIANS
THE JUNGLES OF NEW GUINEA
MACARTHUR'S RETURN

WAR IN EUROPE
BLITZKRIEG
THE FALL OF FRANCE
THE BATTLE OF BRITAIN
BATTLES IN THE BALKANS

Coming Soon

WAR IN EUROPE
NORTH AFRICAN STRUGGLE

Avon Books are available at special quantity discounts for bulk purchases for sales promotions, premiums, fund raising or educational use. Special books, or book excerpts, can also be created to fit specific needs.

For details write or telephone the office of the Director of Special Markets, Avon Books, Dept. FP, 1350 Avenue of the Americas, New York, New York 10019, 1-800-238-0658.

WAR IN THE PACIFIC
VOLUME IX
IWO JIMA

EDWIN P. HOYT

AVON BOOKS • NEW YORK

If you purchased this book without a cover, you should be aware that this book is stolen property. It was reported as "unsold and destroyed" to the publisher, and neither the author nor the publisher has received any payment for this "stripped book."

WAR IN THE PACIFIC, VOLUME 9: IWO JIMA is an original publication of Avon Books. This work has never before appeared in book form.

AVON BOOKS
A division of
The Hearst Corporation
1350 Avenue of the Americas
New York, New York 10019

Copyright © 1992 by Edwin P. Hoyt
Published by arrangement with the author
Library of Congress Catalog Card Number: 92-90336
ISBN: 0-380-76582-9

All rights reserved, which includes the right to reproduce this book or portions thereof in any form whatsoever except as provided by the U.S. Copyright Law. For information address Avon Books.

First Avon Books Printing: December 1992

AVON TRADEMARK REG. U.S. PAT. OFF. AND IN OTHER COUNTRIES, MARCA REGISTRADA, HECHO EN U.S.A.

Printed in the U.S.A.

RA 10 9 8 7 6 5 4 3 2 1

My interest in Iwo Jima began at the end of World War II when I met Keither Wheeler of the *Chicago Times*, who had been wounded while covering the battle for the island. We discussed Iwo Jima, and I read with great interest my friend Robert Sherrod's war reports from the island. But this book about Iwo Jima is based largely on the marine histories of the battle, and several other battle histories. I am grateful to Olga G. Hoyt, as always, for her editing, management of relations with the publishers, and her encouragement in difficult times.

CONTENTS

1. The American Plan — 1
2. The American Assault Force — 9
3. The Defenses of Iwo Jima — 13
4. Softening Up for Iwo Jima — 20
5. The Landings — 28
6. Crossing the Island — 39
7. The Airfield — 47
8. The Twenty-Fifth Marines Had a Little Problem... — 55
9. "The Most Savage and the Most Costly Battle" — 65
10. Night — 70
11. The Second Phase — 77
12. The Most Dangerous Game — 91
13. The Capture of Mt. Suribachi — 103
14. The Medics — 110
15. The Main Attack — 113
16. And in the Second Week... — 126
17. The Meatgrinder — 139
18. Attrition — 149
19. But a Limited Success — 163
20. A Little Help — 173
21. Pressure — 181
22. The Waste of the Azusa Unit — 188
23. And the Fighting Went On and On — 191

Notes — 198

Bibliography — 204

Index — 206

CHAPTER ONE

The American Plan

After the Russo-Japanese War ended, suddenly the strategic considerations in the Pacific changed. Before the war, the Japanese had pictured Russia as their basic enemy. After that war, the enemy changed and became the United States, at least partly because of Japanese resentment against President Theodore Roosevelt's refusal, as arbiter of the treaty ending the Russo-Japanese War, to give the Japanese the cash reparations they demanded from Russia. The Japanese army and navy were counting on that money to rebuild their military machine, and when they did not get it, both services had hard going until World War I brought big military budgets. In all that time they nursed their animosities toward the United States, and the U.S. Fleet became a primary target of their war games.

The Americans responded by making Japan the object of Plan Orange, which was the Pacific war plan. It envisaged an attack on the American possessions in the western Pacific: Guam, the Philippines, and perhaps Samoa and Midway, and the loss of these possessions. After that the American fleet would fight its way back across the central Pacific, hopping from island chain to chain, until the victorious forces reached Japan.

The Japanese attack on Pearl Harbor set that plan in motion, except that world events and the Japanese planning combined to make several sharp changes in it.

First of all, a few days after the Pearl Harbor attack, Prime Minister Winston Churchill and the British military and naval chiefs rushed to Washington, where they persuaded President

2 IWO JIMA

Franklin D. Roosevelt to set aside the natural American inclination to fight the Japanese who had attacked the United States and to devote the major American military effort to the defeat of Hitler until this was accomplished. The American chiefs of staff were not prepared for this idea, and were quickly overwhelmed by the British, who had been preparing for some time. Later the American leaders were to say that they had been bulldozed into accepting the British plan. But it was accepted, and it became American military policy, much to the dismay of General Douglas MacArthur, the commander of American forces in the Far East, who had set out to conduct a defense of the Philippines, expecting assistance from the United States to arrive within a few weeks after the initial Japanese attack. Instead he got nothing but a few submarine loads of ammunition and medical supplies. At least one big convoy that was heading west from America was stopped in mid-ocean and diverted. The initial army plans had been to reinforce the air forces and land forces in the Philippines, and just before the Pearl Harbor attack a flight of B-17s destined for Clark Field had been dispatched from California. They arrived in Pearl Harbor in the middle of the raid. But they were the last to be sent off, and they did not reach their destination.

General MacArthur had conducted a strategic retreat from Manila and the southern Philippines, concentrating his forces in the rugged Bataan peninsula, where the terrain favored the defense. And there the Americans had held out, conducting the most spirited defense operations in the whole Far East, until starvation and disease had laid them low. In April 1942, they had been forced to surrender Bataan, and in May the fortress of Corregidor, which gave the Japanese control of the Philippines. All that remained were a large number of troops, in the southern islands for the most part, who joined with Filipinos to conduct guerilla operations that continued throughout the Pacific War.

Meanwhile American eyes were turned largely toward Europe, and in the Pacific a holding action was ordered. But all this came to a crisis in the summer of 1942. The Japanese had expanded at will, apparently. They had captured Hong Kong on Christmas Day 1941, and Singapore in February

1942, weeks ahead of schedule. In February, they had moved into the Dutch East Indies, and in March had conquered them, expanding as far afield as Rabaul on New Britain Island, a big base which could be a jumping off point for even further expansions into the British half of New Guinea Island and Australia. The Japanese had their eyes on all these places, plus Samoa, Fiji, and the French New Hebrides.

The first intimation of the second round of Japanese expansion came to the Americans in the spring of 1942, with the Japanese invasion of Lae and Salamaua on the shore of New Guinea. Then early in May the Japanese invaded little Tulagi Island, on the edge of Florida Island of the Solomons chain, where overnight they established a seaplane base. The Americans, who had two task forces with carriers in that area, attacked the base and destroyed the seaplanes, but the installation remained. A few hours later, the Americans and a Japanese carrier force fought the battle of the Coral Sea. The direct cause of the battle was a Japanese attempt to send a convoy to attack Port Moresby in New Guinea. The convoy was called back because of the battle and never did arrive. The Americans lost the fleet carrier *Lexington* in this battle, but the Japanese lost a light carrier and their two new carriers, *Shokaku* and *Zuikaku*, suffered such damage that they could not participate in the battle of Midway a few weeks later, a fact which helped turn that battle around from what appeared to be an easy Japanese victory to a stunning Japanese defeat with the loss of four carriers. This loss was to have serious effects on the rest of the air war in the Pacific. The Japanese never did recover their carrier superiority, and the Americans, who had started with far fewer carriers than the Japanese, built them furiously in 1942 and 1943, and by 1944 were vastly superior in carrier forces as well as all other fleet forces in the Pacific.

In 1942, however, the outlook was still bleak for the Allies in the Central and South Pacific. Admiral Isoroku Yamamoto had started the building of a major air base on the island of Guadalcanal. One day, Admiral Ernest J. King, commander of the American fleet, discovered the existence of this airfield, only half completed. His reaction was electric. He insisted that

4 IWO JIMA

something had to be done immediately to stop this expansion, and although Generals George C. Marshall and Henry H. Arnold and Admiral William D. Leahy, the other members of the Joint Chiefs of Staff were surprised, King's insistence convinced them, and the plans were hurriedly made for an assault by the American Marine 1st Division on the island of Guadalcanal.

Until this time, the American effort in the Pacific had been largely defensive, punctuated by several air raids that gave the Japanese concern. One of these was the raid by American forces on the Marshall Islands in March 1942, which proved to Admiral Yamamoto that the American fleet was far from dead. (In the raid, the naval commander of the Marshalls, a rear admiral, was killed.) Another raid that troubled the Japanese was the raid by Lieutenant Colonel James Doolittle, leading sixteen B-25 medium army bombers from a carrier to raid Japan itself. The raid did very little physical damage, but a great deal of emotional damage to the Japanese military leaders, who saw that at some time in the future such raids might become commonplace.

This was a major reason for Admiral Yamamoto's insistence on the Midway operation, to draw out and destroy the American fleet.

When that operation failed and the Americans moved into Guadalcanal, the war changed. For months it was a touch and go proposition, with the Japanese winning almost all the naval engagements and maintaining control of the air. But gradually the Americans gained air superiority. Meanwhile the marines clung tenaciously to their exposed position on Guadalcanal and ultimately triumphed on the ground. After the Japanese evacuated Guadalcanal in February 1943, the war changed, and Japan for the first time went on the defensive.

Japan's defense perimeter was once planned in such grandiose terms that it would extend from the Aleutian Islands to Samoa, thence around the Dutch East Indies and just north of Australia, to India. But by 1944 the Allies had whittled away the southern section of this line and taken back the Aleutians. The Japanese contracted, making first the Palau Islands their center point of defense and then retreating to the Marianas

The American Plan

and the Philippines. But the Marianas fell to the Allies in the summer of 1944, and then the Japanese made the most major reorganization of their defenses since the war began.

From the beginning, the Japanese navy had sought the decisive battle with the American fleet, which they hoped would leave the American fleet crippled and force the Americans to the peace table, at which Japan could hope for acceptance of the territorial gains she had made and a free hand in China. But with the fall of the Marianas, several new considerations emerged. Primary was the knowledge that one reason the Americans had taken the Marianas was to provide air bases for the new bomber they had already introduced into west China. From there they had bombed Kyushu and Manchuria. These were the B-29 Superfortresses, with the capacity to bomb Japan. From Marianas bases they could reach Tokyo and points on the Kanto plain, the main manufacturing area of the Japanese.

So with the fall of the Marianas the defense planners sought the decisive battle more desperately than before, and when the next invasion threatened the China coast, Taiwan or the Philippines the Japanese countered with the Sho I operation, in which they would risk their entire fleet to try to destroy the American fleet. Already their carrier forces had been reduced in the battle of the Philippine Sea at the time of the Marianas invasion and were less effective than the American force had been at the beginning of the war. In August, September, and October, Admiral William F. Halsey ranged around the Philippines and the Palau islands and Taiwan with the vastly increased Third Fleet and Task Force 38, the carrier unit, destroying Japanese naval and air facilities.

Meanwhile, the American Pacific strategy changed sharply. After the Marianas battle the Joint Chiefs of Staff had taken a new cognizance of General MacArthur. While the navy had been leading the assault on the central Pacific, MacArthur had been doggedly working his way up the New Guinea coast, until in the middle of the summer of 1944, he was standing on the Vogelkap, at the top of New Guinea. Now he could argue anew that the shortest road to Tokyo was through the Philippines.

6 IWO JIMA

MacArthur did so argue in the summer of 1944. The way was open for a new receptivity in Washington about how to proceed against Japan. By the middle of the summer, Washington believed that the European war was nearly over. In Britain Field Marshal Bernard Law Montgomery said as much. So the feeling in Washington was that it was time to devote more attention to the Pacific.

If that were true, then the basic dispute between the army and the navy over the approach to Japan had to be settled. The navy wanted to go to the China coast or to Taiwan, and then to Japan. The army backed General MacArthur's view that the next approach ought to be through the Philippines. At a meeting at Pearl Harbor with President Roosevelt and Admiral Chester W. Nimitz, MacArthur propounded his theory vigorously, and shrewdly paid particular attention to the international political implications of the attack through the Philippines, pointing out that the United States was redeeming its promise to the Filipinos to free them from the Japanese and then give them the total freedom they had been promised.

Meanwhile, early in 1944, the Japanese had moved the majority of their combined fleet down to Lingga Roads, off Singapore, which seemed to the British to be a threat to India. The Japanese had also begun an advance in China from Hangzhou in central China along the railroad to Hanoi, Indochina, and had begun rolling up Chinese airfields which were used by the U.S. Fourteenth Air Force. This was part of a plan of the Japanese Imperial General Headquarters to tighten the Japanese defenses of Asia proper, making it possible to move supplies and troops overland from Manchuria to Burma. Obviously this threat was important.

Because of this and the other considerations of political and military futures, the Joint Chiefs of Staff agreed to invade first the Philippines, and then Formosa or the China coast.

The first planning called for the American assault to be on the southern island of Mindanao, but Admiral Halsey found in his movements around the Philippines that Japanese defenses on Mindanao were very slight, and not worth bothering about. So the decision was changed and Leyte in the central Philippines was substituted for Mindanao.

Then came the actual invasion of Leyte, and the Japanese responded with the call for the Sho I operation. Their entire naval force and their entire navy air force were called into play. In air battles around Formosa and the Philippines, the navy air force was so reduced that by the time the American troops landed on Leyte, in the third week of October, the Japanese naval air forces in the Philippines were reduced to about 200 planes. Admiral Takejiro Ohnishi, who was called upon to defend the Philippines and participate in the Sho I operation, decided that all he could do was begin the suicide operations that he had long envisaged as a last resort. That way his fighter pilots could become effective bombers and their airplanes would become bombs, hopefully to destroy carriers.

From this point on, the Japanese naval forces were so slight that they would not make a squadron, and so the major Japanese naval weapon became the *kamikaze* plane.

Meanwhile, the defenses of the Japanese empire also contracted. When the Marianas were captured, the Japanese saw immediately that the Americans would soon want an island base for fighters to protect the B-29s on their 1,400-mile flight from Saipan and Tinian to Tokyo, and also as a base for the landing of crippled bombers. How right they were! Major General Curtis LeMay, who had earned his reputation in the Eighth Air Force for ferocious bombing campaigns, had been sent to the Pacific, and was operating that spring of 1944 out of west China. When Saipan was captured, he moved to the Marianas. The first American B-29 raid from Saipan was successful when it was sent off at the end of November, but thereafter there was nothing but trouble. The Americans had the air bases from which to reach Japan, but the Japanese had dozens of airfields between the Marianas and Japan, and the Americans had none. Therefore fighters from Iwo Jima and several other islands could attack the American bombers on the way to the target and on the way home, and fighters from Japan could attack them over the target and follow them out to sea. LeMay complained that his missions were being chewed to pieces. The

8 IWO JIMA

answer was that the B-29s had to have fighter support, and it had to be placed somewhere that long-distance fighters could be useful. Fortunately the Americans had the airplane, the P-51 Mustang. What they needed was a base about halfway between Saipan and the Japanese homeland.

The island of Iwo Jima is situated almost exactly halfway between Tokyo and Saipan, and the Japanese quite correctly guessed that Iwo Jima would soon be an American objective.

In September 1944, then, the Japanese set out to make Iwo Jima as difficult to attack as would be humanly possible.

CHAPTER TWO

The American Assault Force

The capture of the Marianas Islands began with a meeting of the British and American Combined Chiefs of Staff in Casablanca in January 1943, when Admiral Ernest J. King observed that the Marianas were a key to unlocking the attack on Japan, because they were on the main line of Japanese communications. He and other naval officers were looking at the Marianas as the logical point of attack on the inner perimeter of the Japanese home defenses. The Marianas would also make fine bases for submarines, long-range bombers, and resupply of surface task forces.

The naval plan then was to defeat Japan without invasion, by destroying her communications, and her submarine force. This would deprive her of the rubber, oil, and other goods of war that she had secured by her "strike south" to take the Dutch East Indies and Malaya.

Admiral King kept after this point. By the Quebec Conference of 1943 he had convinced General George C. Marshall and General Henry H. Arnold that the Marianas were the key to the defense of the Central Pacific for Japan. General Arnold remembered all this, and when he began having difficulties mounting B-29 bombing attacks from China bases, he thought about the Marianas again. Even before that time U.S. Air Force planners had called attention to the Marianas as the ideal base for the bombing of Japan by

10 IWO JIMA

B-29s with their 1,500-mile range, carrying 10,000 pounds of bombs.

On July 14, 1944, General Arnold recommended that Iwo Jima be seized to strengthen his hand in the Marianas, which were just being occupied. He wanted B-29 bases there, but it was 1,400 miles from Saipan to Tokyo, and lying halfway between were the Bonin Islands, which gave the Japanese air bases and deprived the B-29s of support bases and emergency landing fields. The capture of the Bonins—or at least their neutralization and the capture of one of them—would go a long way toward the defeat of Japan. The new P-51 fighter planes with their long range would be ideal for the support of the B-29s from a base in the Bonins. In other words, all the difficulties that the Twentieth Air Force was experiencing in the fall of 1944 at Saipan were known to the Air Force earlier, but it was a question of logistics. One could not do everything at once. The full extent of the difficulties of the B-29s was not really understood until they began operating from the Marianas bases. So the planning had taken a bit of time.

In October, even as General MacArthur was getting ready to move into the Philippines, Rear Admiral Forrest Sherman was supervising the planning for the invasion of Iwo Jima. Admiral Raymond Spruance would be commander of the whole expedition. Under him Vice Admiral Richmond Kelly Turner would command the expeditionary force, and Lieutenant General Holland M. Smith of the Marine Corps would command the Marine landing force. The troops would be the Third Marine Division under Major General Graves B. Erskine, and the Fourth Marine Division under Major General Clifton B. Cates, and the newly formed Fifth Marine Division under Major General Keller E. Rockey. Overall command was in the hands of Major General Harry Schmidt, commander of the Marine V Amphibious Corps. Admiral Turner's subordinate commanders were Rear Admiral Harry W. Hill and Rear Admiral William H. P. Blandy.

Also in support of the whole operation was Vice Admiral Marc A. Mitscher's Task Force 58, the fast carrier force, and the logistic support group, headed by Rear Admiral Donald B. Beary.

Some new techniques of speeding-up operations would be used, the most important of which was the transfer of planes at sea. Five escort carriers were used to carry replacement planes for the big carriers.

One of the important aspects of the Iwo Jima campaign that had not existed in the past was the extensive ability of the American forces to use land-based aircraft in support of operations. Hitherto, in the Central Pacific the enemy bases had been so far from one another that the Americans had to rely largely on carrier-based aircraft. In the South Pacific they had relied on the Guadalcanal air force and the U.S. Fifth Air Force in Australia and New Guinea for operational support, but this was a whole new situation. At the end of 1944, Lieutenant General Millard F. Harmon became commander of all land-based aviation in the Pacific, including army, air force, and navy.

The Marianas became famous because of the B-29 bases, but there were many other air bases there as well, and the Seventh Army Air Force operated from them. Major General Willis H. Hale commanded that air force. Its major task at this moment was to neutralize Iwo Jima and all bases that might support the Japanese in the Iwo Jima operation. Truk was a major target, so were Ponape, Wotje and Wake and Marcus islands. On August 10, the first B-24s based on Saipan hit Iwo Jima. Thereafter Iwo Jima was bombed by B-24s almost every day that weather permitted.

The first B-29s arrived in the Marianas on October 12, 1944. The Japanese knew they were coming and began to attack. Their early attacks were not very successful but after the first B-29 raid from Saipan they made a great effort. The B-29 raid was on November 24. Three days later, two twin-engined Japanese bombers came in and bombed, destroying one B-29 and damaging eleven others. Later that day fifteen single-engine planes attacked, destroying three more B-29s and damaging two. After that, raids continued until January, destroying eleven more B-29s and damaging six. Soon enough Iwo Jima was suspected as the staging point for these raids on Saipan, and Admiral Nimitz ordered that the island be given top priority for bombardment. So in late December and January Iwo Jima became the prime target not only of the land-based bombers and fighters, but also of sea bombardment. A heavy cruiser force attacked Iwo Jima on December 8 for seventy minutes.

The Seventh Air Force was then ordered to keep Iwo Jima neutralized so that bombers could not use its airfields. But this was easier said than done, and the Japanese paid more visits to Saipan. On Christmas Eve twenty-five Japanese planes struck, destroying four B-29s.

So the American cruisers went back on December 27. Again, on January 25, they hit Iwo Jima, and the heavy bombers and fighters also struck the island. This time the sea bombardment lasted for two hours.

And beginning on the last day of January, for two weeks Seventh Air Force B-24s bombed Iwo Jima day and night. B-29s joined the raids on three occasions, dropping 370 tons of bombs. The result was that for ten weeks before the assault on Iwo Jima, it was bombed or bombarded nearly every day. One might have thought that everything alive on the island had been destroyed. But the fact was that the Japanese installations were so well planned and well built that the only damage was to the airfields, and these were repaired every night after they had been bombed. Aircraft continued to use them up until the last, when the American fleet and the American carriers came.

In spite of the evidence of the ability of the Japanese to withstand the bombardment, the Americans continued to believe that the capture of Iwo Jima was only going to take a few days. After all, they had the experience of Tarawa, Kwajalein, Eniwetak, Saipan, Tinian, Guam, and Peleliu to go on. That was quite correct, but they had not yet seen Iwo Jima. They had something more to learn.

CHAPTER THREE

The Defenses of Iwo Jima

In the early years of the Pacific War, the major Japanese base in the Bonin Islands was Chichi Jima, which had been a Japanese navy base since 1914. The island of Iwo Jima, the central island in the Volcano group of the Bonins, was inhabited before World War II by only about 1,100 Japanese civilians who raised sugar and pineapples and ran a sugar mill and a sulphur factory. But in 1943 the defenders of Iwo Jima had another look; the civilians were evacuated and the island turned to defense purposes. At that point, Iwo Jima had only a single airstrip and garrison of about 1,500 troops. In March 1944, the buildup of Iwo Jima and the other islands in the Bonin chain began in earnest. Before summer came, the garrison had been increased to 5,000 troops and artillery, and many machine guns had been brought in. A navy guard had been added, with a dozen coastal defense guns of 120mm caliber and even larger. A dozen heavy antiaircraft guns and many 25mm antiaircraft guns had also been added to the arsenal. Two thousand naval men manned the antiaircraft defenses and the garrison was gradually increased to 21,000 men. The commander of the defense was Rear Admiral Toshinosuke Ichimaru.

Even before the Saipan invasion, Tokyo was determined to build up Iwo Jima. Late in May 1944, the 109th Infantry Division was organized and sent to Iwo Jima under the command of Lieutenant General Tadamichi Kuribayashi. Like the Allies, the

14 IWO JIMA

Japanese had to decide among several of the islands, Ie Shima, Chichi Jima and Iwo Jima. Correctly they decided that Iwo Jima was the most likely to be invaded and they acted accordingly.

When General Kuribayashi arrived on Iwo Jima, he was greeted by a delegation of a hundred school children. That indicated to him that the state of the defense was far too weak; this was no place for children. He set about righting that by removing all the civilians to Chichi Jima, except for a few who were inducted into the army, and by demanding increases in all aspects of the defense of the island.

On June 15, the island had its first serious attack, when seven carriers struck the island in connection with the softening up of the Marianas. For two days the Americans blasted the airfields of Iwo Jima and knocked out most of the aircraft around the island.

More Japanese troops were brought in. Since Iwo Jima did not have a harbor, the troops were brought by ship to Chichi Jima and then by smaller craft to Iwo Jima. The ships came from Japan to Chichi Jima and were unloaded at night there. The troops and supplies then were trucked into the hills, and the supplies were dispersed in the woods, while the men were housed in one of several long highway tunnels. The next evening the supplies and troops for Iwo Jima were brought down to the harbor and loaded aboard small vessels. These craft then set sail for Haha Jima, on the way to Iwo, which they reached early the next morning. They holed up on Haha Jima during the day, and that night went on to Iwo Jima, where they were unloaded.

Thousands of bags of cement and tons of reinforcing rods of steel also were brought in this way.

All this activity engendered much interest by American submarines, and several Japanese ships bearing reinforcements and supplies for the buildup of the Iwo Jima garrison were sunk. On July 18, the American submarine *Cobia* sank the *Nisshu Maru*, which was enroute from Japan to Iwo Jima, carrying the 26th Tank Regiment. Most of the troops were saved, but twenty-eight tanks went down. Lieutenant Colonel Takeichi Nishi, the commander of the regiment, later went back to Tokyo and made arrangements for more tanks to be sent to Iwo Jima.

The Defenses of Iwo Jima   15

Iwo Jima is an odd piece of real estate which was described by one marine as "not worth fifty cents." It is only two and a half miles wide and five miles long. Its surface is covered by what looks like ordinary gray sand but is not. It is gray volcanic ash, much lighter than sand in weight, on top of a crust of hard lava. To walk on Iwo Jima is an effort. To run is impossible. The island is shaped something like a pork chop, with its old volcano Mount Suribachi at the extreme narrow south end. Suribachi, which is 560 feet above sea level, was a perfect lookout station. From around its crater ridge one could see every point of the island. Airfield No. 1 was placed about one-third up the island, Airfield No. 2 farther north than that, and Airfield No. 3 was under construction at the northern end of the island. The slopes of Mt. Suribachi contained a maze of gun positions, which included coastal artillery, field guns, mortars and machine guns. Each of these had its own system of caves and tunnels. The caves protected the equipment, the ammunition, and the personnel. The tunnels led from one position to another. Repair shops and service facilities were included underground.

One main line of defense crossed the island between No. 1 Airfield and No. 2 Airfield, and here again was a network of dug-in positions for artillery, mortars, and machine guns. All these, too, were connected by interlocking tunnels and big caves.

The second line of defense led between the No. 2 Airfield and Motoyama village in the center of the island's bulge. This bulge had an even more intricate system of caves and tunnels, five levels deep in some places, and few of them less than thirty feet underground. Each cave usually had several entrances. A mortar could be set up, fired for a few rounds, and then moved back underground and out to another entrance to start firing again. The Japanese gun positions were made of reinforced concrete four to six feet deep and everything was camouflaged, using natural materials to the best possible advantage.

General Kuribayashi's orders from the Imperial Army were to transform Iwo Jima into a real fortress and be prepared to defend it to the death. He followed his orders implicitly.

16 IWO JIMA

There were to be no *banzai* charges on the beaches, or any heroics. Consulting the records, he decided that the idea of trying to stand on the water's edge would not work. He wanted an in-depth defense. He proposed to let the enemy get onto the beaches, and then to chew them to pieces with artillery fire and automatic weapons. He issued orders against any counterattacks except tanks, and tanks were given high priority as targets.

There was some argument with General Kuribayashi's decisions, and ultimately he got rid of nineteen officers who either refused to obey his commands or spent so much time arguing that he felt better off without them.

The enemy was to be avoided as far as possible, and losses were to be prevented during enemy bombardment and bombing. The watchword was that this was "*hissi tatukai*," or battle to the death. The Japanese responsibility was to create attrition in the enemy ranks, and if necessary to defend a corner of the island to the death. The one hope of survival, discussed but believed by no one on the island, was that the defense would be so fierce that the Americans would ultimately back off. That was what the soldiers wrote home to their families, but no one really believed it. Soon the men of Iwo Jima were resigned to the fact that they had no chance of survival, and they began to call themselves "the underground troops."

The general drew his plan of defense very carefully, taking advantage of all he could discover about the previous island defenses of Japan in this war. Before he was finished he had built 750 installations, including more than a hundred guns larger than 75mm. He had 90 large mortars and rocket launchers as large as 320mm which fired 500-pound rockets. He had 130 howitzers, 69 antitank guns, and 240 machine guns of 20mm and larger. He had 24 tanks, most of them dug in. There were more than 200 beach installations, which included blockhouses with five-foot-thick walls. Behind the beaches were nearly a hundred concrete pillboxes and more than 30 covered artillery emplacements.

In August 1944, the tempo of attacks on Iwo Jima increased with the coming of the American Seventh Air Force to the

The Defenses of Iwo Jima   17

Marianas. The Force sent B-24s to bomb Iwo Jima, and they came often. The Iwo Jima antiaircraft batteries fired on them and sometimes scored hits, and the Japanese fighter planes on Iwo Jima were really dangerous.

On August 14, thirteen B-24s struck Iwo Jima's Airfield No. 1. Two of the B-24s were hit. The first plane made it back to its base with 150 bullet holes. The second B-24 was hit repeatedly by fighters, and the pilot was wounded, but he managed to fly the aircraft back, almost to Saipan, before the controls gave way and he told the men to parachute. Several of them did, but only one of them survived. The others went down with the plane, but the pilot and a radio operator managed to get clear of the plane before it sank.

By September, the Iwo Jima defenses were being built with great speed. There were then about 15,000 men on the island. The 109th Infantry Division was still the main organization, but there were several independent battalions and a mixed regiment.

In November, the Japanese stepped up their training program, concentrating on building fields of fire for their weapons and on sniper training for the infantry.

General Kuribayashi prepared his men for the ordeal that was to come. His general order was calculated to instill the *samurai* spirit in the men: "The Japanese spirit is based on 3,000 years of history and a respect for God and our ancestors. We must purify our mental condition and increase this spirit, destroying the enemy that is trying to overrun it and making the spirit known to the world. We are now in the front line for the national defense. We must do everything we can for the emperor, for the personnel already perished in the war, and for the people of the homeland."

All over the island officers posted his set of "courageous vows."

"Above all, we shall dedicate ourselves and our entire strength to the defense of the island; we shall grasp bombs, charge enemy tanks and destroy them; we shall infiltrate into the midst of the enemy and annihilate them; with every salvo we will without fail kill the enemy. Each man will make it his duty to kill ten of the enemy before dying; until we are destroyed to the last man we shall harass the enemy with guerilla tactics."

General Kuribayashi was obdurate about maintaining the utmost strength until the last.

What were they to do with the new tanks that came in? Colonel Nishi, a cavalry officer and Olympic gold medal horseman converted to an armored officer, wanted to maintain the utmost mobility, but in the end almost all of the tanks were buried, with only their turrets and guns showing.

General Kuribayashi's headquarters was located at the north end of the island, underneath a blockhouse that was the communications center of the island. This blockhouse was built of reinforced concrete with five-foot-thick walls and a ten-foot-thick roof. Seventy-five feet below the radio room was a system of caves and tunnels in which the general and his staff had their quarters, small concrete walled rooms, with light furnished only by candles.

In January 1945, the Imperial General Headquarters devised a new defense for Japan. The American landings on Luzon indicated that it would not be long before the Allies came even closer to the homeland, perhaps through China, Okinawa, or Taiwan. All these places were to be defended to the death, to preserve the Japanese home islands from attack as long as possible. Except for the garrisons that existed on these islands and in these places, no plans were made for reinforcement. Supplies and weapons stopped coming in. All troops and most weapons were to be saved for the actual defense of the homeland when that time came.

Army and navy officials met almost interminably to try to work out a joint defense system, but the best they could come up with was a plan under which the navy would continue to defend the sea offshore, including the islands near Japan, while the army responsibility would be to garrison the islands with troops and to act when the enemy actually landed. The exception was in the air, where the army, which had more aircraft than the navy, agreed to participate in the attacks on the enemy when they came to Japan and the nearby islands. This assistance offer was welcomed by the Japanese navy but not given too much

The Defenses of Iwo Jima 19

importance, because the army fliers continued to be deficient in navigation and their attack methods were not designed for assault on warships.

As a result of the army-navy discussions, it was decided that the first line of defense of Japan would be the *kamikaze* suicide corps, and the naval air force and army air force were reorganized to that end. The navy defense was split into two sections. One, the Third Air Fleet, under Vice Admiral Kimpei Teraoka, was made responsible for training and the defense of Oahu. The second element, the Fifth Air Fleet, under Vice Admiral Matome Ugaki, was made responsible for the defense of Kyushu and the southern islands, including Iwo Jima and Okinawa. On February 10, 1945, Ugaki was supposed to visit the imperial palace for the ceremony of his appointment to this important task by the emperor himself, but an afternoon air raid by B-29s caused the cancellation of the ceremony. Nevertheless, his appointment stood. He began immediately to make preparations for the strengthening of the suicide elements of the Fifth Air Fleet. On February 14, Admiral Ugaki took over at Kanoya air base in southern Kyushu. That day, search planes of his air force found about a hundred enemy vessels west of Saipan sailing north, which meant toward the southern islands and Japan. This was part of the Iwo Jima invasion force, although Admiral Ugaki did not then know it.

Ugaki suspected that the enemy was going to attack the islands of Japan preparatory to invading Iwo Jima, and he was right. On February 16, the Americans struck, with carrier planes in three waves, not only in the Kanto area of Japan, but at Iwo Jima and Harami and Hamamatsu. Admiral Ugaki wanted to respond, but he had not yet had enough time to organize his forces, and did not have the strength ready to do so.

So the battle for Iwo Jima was joined before the landing forces reached the island itself.

CHAPTER FOUR

Softening Up for Iwo Jima

After more than three months of experience with the new Japanese tactic of suicide air warfare, the American carrier fleet had made some changes in its methods of operation. Vice Admiral Marc Mitscher's Task Force 58 consisted of four regular carrier task groups and one special night carrier task group. The total number of carriers involved was sixteen, along with eight battleships, five cruisers, nine light cruisers, and seventy-seven destroyers. They set out on a multiple mission on February 10, 1945, to soften up Iwo Jima, to try to prevent the Japanese from reinforcing the air forces involved that might hamper the Iwo Jima operations, and to attack Japan's airfields, thus trying to stop up the pipeline of air defense.

The carrier air groups had been reorganized since the advent of the *kamikaze* attacks to strengthen the fighter quotient. On the fleet carriers, fighters now made up two-thirds of the force, a drop in the attack capacity of the carriers necessary to protect against suicide planes. To make up for this, some of the fighters also carried bombs for attack purposes.

When the task force left Ulithi on February 10, it headed for the Marianas and Bonins, and on February 12, it stopped off for an invasion rehearsal with the Third Marine Division on Tinian Island. On February 14, the task force fuelled at sea. Care was taken to avoid detection by the Japanese, and although other elements of the Iwo Jima invasion fleet were seen, including the force of escort carriers that had been sent out to help protect the invasion, the task force itself was not observed.

On February 15, a scouting line of five destroyers moved out ahead of the carrier force to dispose of any picket boats that might be encountered on the run into the shores of Japan, and the antisubmarine air patrol worked over the area ahead of the force. At seven o'clock in the evening the run in toward the Japanese shore began at high speed from about six hundred miles out through very thick weather, which helped keep the Japanese off guard. By 6 A.M. on February 16, the task force had reached its launching point about 125 miles southeast of Tokyo but not much more than 50 miles off the Honshu shore.

The weather was anything but admirable. The ceiling was only 4,000 feet, and broken clouds began at 1,000 feet, with rain squalls and snow. A stiff wind was blowing. In this bad weather several fighter sweeps were launched to hit the airfields around Tokyo.

What was bad weather for the Americans was also bad weather for the Japanese, and not many enemy fighters were flying. The first air sweep from the carriers *Lexington*, *Hancock* and *San Jacinto* over the Chiba peninsula did encounter fighter opposition. About a hundred Japanese fighters arose to meet the incoming American planes, and the American fighters claimed to have shot down forty of them. American pilots returned to announce that the Japanese seemed reluctant to fight. This represented a lack of skill and training rather than inclination, although the Americans did not know it. The fighters from the *Essex*, *Bunker Hill* and *Cowpens* went to Tokyo, where they encountered virtually no opposition. So the planes came back to their carriers, gassed up, rearmed, and set off again. All day long the American aircraft hovered over the Japanese shore, covering the airfields and keeping the Japanese planes on the ground.

Another reason for the failure of the Japanese to respond with strong opposition was a general unreadiness of the Japanese forces for this attack, although they knew it was bound to come soon. The Third Air Fleet, which was responsible for the defense of the Tokyo area, was in the process of transferring some of its planes to the Fifth Air Fleet. The result was that the American planes, by Japanese count, destroyed 150 planes on the ground in addition to the planes destroyed in the air. The Americans claimed to have destroyed 540 planes on the ground and in the air. The American losses were eighty-eight planes.

The purpose of the American raids was twofold: to destroy aircraft that might be sent to Iwo Jima to interfere with the landings, and to destroy aircraft facilities. In the latter connection, they hit the Ota and Koizumi aircraft factories in the Tokyo area and did serious damage to both. They might have done more damage except that the weather was so bad that many bombing pilots did not find their targets and spent their bombs on the airfields instead. Runways were cratered, which did not have much long term effect, but some buildings and aircraft installations at the fields were destroyed, which did have a real effect.

The shock value of the raid was terrific. Imperial General Headquarters feared early on that this was a full-scale invasion and called the alert for Sho No 3, the invasion of Honshu. When it was discovered that there were no landing forces involved this alert was called off. The Japanese lack of preparedness shocked Admiral Matome Ugaki, who observed in a diary he was keeping that it seemed that the army had learned nothing in the last few months about defenses and the need for them.

After the first day's air strikes, the American fleet maneuvered off the Japanese coast all night, and the next day the American carrier planes struck the area again. On this second day the results were not so spectacular because the Japanese refused to come out, and instead of fighting concealed their planes on the ground. This was the basic Japanese policy of defense, to preserve their fighting strength for the actual invasion of Japan.

As Admiral Ugaki wrote in his diary:

"The Combined Fleet endured its challenge and remained quiet in directing the war."

But it did invoke a plan for an operation to be carried out later when the carrier fleet would return to Ulithi. Admiral Ugaki was

Softening Up for Iwo Jima 23

ordered to prepare for Operation Tan, which would be an attack by twenty-four twin-engined bombers on the carrier fleet. With the unreasoning hope that now characterized most Japanese operations, they expected to "destroy" the effectiveness of the carrier fleet.

Meanwhile another amphibious group under Rear Admiral William H. P. Blandy moved off Iwo Jima on February 16, and began attacking that island, preparing for the invasion. He had a dozen escort carriers under Rear Admiral C. T. Durgin, and six battleships: the *Idaho*, *Tennessee*, *Nevada*, *Texas*, *Arkansas*, and *New York*. He also had the four cruisers *Chester*, *Pensacola*, *Salt Lake City* and *Tuscaloosa*, the light cruiser *Vicksburg* and sixteen destroyers to begin working over Iwo Jima. The escort carriers were no longer sneezed at in the American navy as they had been before Admiral Thomas Kinkaid began using them to good effect when he could not get the loan of the fleet carrier force. The four hundred planes these dozen escort carriers could mount could do an enormous amount of damage.

The Blandy force arrived off Iwo Jima at six o'clock on the morning of February 16. The destroyers and destroyer transports formed a screen out to sea from the bombardment ships for the purpose of intercepting any *kamikazes* that came in or any organized bombing attacks that might emanate from the adjacent islands. From an area about 50 miles south of the island, the escort carriers sent up a large combat air patrol and thorough antisubmarine patrol. There were so many aircraft available that the Americans could use them in special ways, and some of the pilots of the carrier *Wake Island* were trained as gunfire spotters, to direct the fire of the ships on the Iwo Jima targets.

The minesweeping of the Iwo Jima area started first at 6:45 A.M. Then a sweep of the Chichi Jima Island airfields was started, but the weather was so poor over the island that it did not succeed. In the bad weather the bombardment of Iwo Jima began. The trouble was that the enemy's facilities were so artfully concealed that the initial bombardment was not very successful, so Admiral Blandy ordered it stopped that morning and directed the ships to fire only when they knew what they were firing at.

All day long the ships bombarded the island when the spotter planes could direct them. The American planes also attacked Japanese planes in the air, and underwater demolition teams (UDT) began preparing the way for landings, checking to be sure there were no underwater obstacles to tear up the landing craft that would be coming a few hours later. The UDT men were harassed by fire from Japanese guns on the island, and the Japanese, in turn, were assaulted by the cruiser *Pensacola*.

But at the end of the day, the big ship men had to admit that on the whole their bombardment had not been very effective. Later they were to learn why: the enemy defenses were so sturdy that area shelling had very little effect. It would take a direct hit on a gun or a pillbox to knock it out, and the camouflage was so good that these installations were virtually unseen in the bad visibility.

The morning of February 17 dawned with much better weather, and the gunners had high hopes of remedying the deficiencies of the day before.

This day the fighter planes ran sweeps against Chichi Jima's important air-fields and port facilities, and B-24 raids against Iwo Jima, besides the fire support from the capital ships around the island. But once again the results were mixed and a little confusing. Early in the day the observers on the cruiser *Pensacola* saw that shore guns were firing on the minesweepers working around the island. The *Pensacola* opened up with her guns, and five minutes later, the firing stopped. The gunner got the idea that they had knocked out the Japanese guns, but this was largely in error. The Japanese were following their preordained fighting plan. Their guns would find a target, fire, and then withdraw into the caves and stop firing. Later they would emerge again at this location or another site connected by tunnels.

This happened to the *Pensacola*. After having "silenced" the guns on which she fired, she suddenly came under fire from a different location and received six hits. They wrecked her combat information center, set fire to a seaplane sitting on the

Softening Up for Iwo Jima 25

starboard catapult, killed seventeen men and wounded ninety-eight. She withdrew from the close support mission for a while to fight fires and take care of casualties.

The men of the ships began to realize what they were up against when they started to bring the UDT team members in to shore in landing craft. The landing craft were supported by seven destroyers and seven LCI (Landing Craft Inventory) gunboats. They fired on the beaches and made their rockets ready to hit the beaches to support the swimmers. But when these men came up to the 1,500-yard line off the beaches, they were suddenly brought under fire from shore guns that had never been noticed before, so artfully were they concealed. The fire came from mortars, automatic weapons and from shore batteries that the ship's gunners could not find. The landing craft began to be hit by the enemy fire, and the swimmers began to suffer casualties. One LCI was sunk and another suffered 60 percent casualties. Altogether in the LCI force forty-four men were killed and 152 wounded.

The heavier ships began to concentrate on the hidden gun positions on the mountain. The battleship *Nevada* fired on one position for two hours, and believed it had knocked the guns out. But the Japanese continued to fire on targets of opportunity, and never remained firing for very long, which made the ships's gunners' tasks more difficult. Just before noon the destroyer *Leutze* was hit by gunfire from the shore, seven men were killed and thirty-four wounded, including the captain of the ship.

The good news that afternoon was that when the UDT men came back from their missions, they reported that no underwater obstacles existed, and they had made maps of the approaches for the use of the landing teams.

This day's afternoon work had to be postponed, because all of the LCIs had been damaged in the morning effort. Late in the afternoon, the destroyers provided support for the reconnaissance of the western beaches, and this was carried out with the same negative results as the other. But this time there were no casualties.

The third day of bombardment, February 18, revealed something new to the Americans. Their shooting had not been very accurate as far as gun positions were concerned in the first two days, but some of their shells had blasted loose camouflage and revealed some of the Japanese gun positions and cave entrances. They were able to get a good view of some of the gun positions around the slopes of Mt. Suribachi. The reason was that the Japanese had made their first miscalculation. When the underwater demolition teams had begun to approach the landing area for their observations, the Japanese had gotten the idea that this was the landing on Iwo Jima, and had thus opened up with many of their previously concealed guns. Now the American ships had a whole day in which to find and silence these guns if they could.

That day, the battleships and cruisers came in close and began to shell. They found blockhouses and pillboxes, and managed to score direct hits and destroy several of them. They fired all day, from 7:45 in the morning until dark. At 9:30 that evening, the ships began to retire to the open sea, and then the Japanese staged an air raid. The destroyer minesweeper *Gamble* was hit by two bombs which caused extensive damage, and killed five men, and wounded nine others. She had to be taken under tow. The destroyer transport *Blessman*, which was the headquarters for one UDT unit, was hit, and she lost forty-two men and twenty-nine were wounded, many of them skilled specialists from the underwater demolition team.

Back in Japan, Admiral Ugaki and the Combined Japanese Fleet assessed the situation. They were puzzled as to why the Americans, with all the force assembled, had not yet staged a landing.

"On the other hand," Admiral Ugaki wrote in his diary, "the enemy is said to have attempted landing on Iwo Jima twice yesterday but has been repulsed each time, and one unidentified ship sunk."

Why had they not followed up?

"Were they waiting for follow-up convoys? How long will the enemy task force operate there?"

The Japanese were pleased to note that their big guns on Iwo Jima had not yet revealed themselves.

Admiral Ugaki also had a special reason for wondering how long the task force would operate around Iwo Jima, for he had been given the responsibility for launching Operation Tan just as soon as the American carriers returned to Ulithi.

That night of February 18, the commanders of the 601st Japanese Air Group and the 801st Air Group visited Admiral Ugaki at his new headquarters at Kanoya air base in southern Kyushu to make arrangements for the coming Operation Tan. All the Japanese officers had great confidence in success.

Next morning the battle for Iwo Jima began in earnest.

CHAPTER FIVE

The Landings

Three marine divisions were scheduled for the Iwo Jima operation, although Admiral Turner and General Smith hoped that they would only have to use two of them, saving the third for the next invasion, of Okinawa.

Three divisions meant between 60,000 and 75,000 men. Each division consisted of riflemen and many specialists, heavy weapons units, transportation units, engineers, signalmen, and even a war dog platoon. On the morning of February 18, two of these divisions, the Fourth and Fifth, were assembled aboard transports off Iwo Jima, with part of the Third Division, but most of that division was held back on other ships: it was the reserve. This was the Fifth Amphibious Corps.

The Third Marine Division had fought at Bougainville and at Guam. The Fourth Marine Division had fought at Roi-Namur in the Marshalls, and at Saipan and Tinian. The Fifth Marine Division was new, and had not fought as a unit, but nearly half the men were veterans of the Pacific campaigns, some of them members of the now disbanded Raider Battalions.

Late in January, the various elements of the invasion fleet for Iwo Jima left Pearl Harbor, and on the second day at sea the marines were told where they were going. On February 5, the convoy anchored at Eniwetak in the Marshall Islands for two days, and then moved on to Saipan on February 11.

Here the Fifth Amphibious Force was split up with the assault waves going aboard LSTs (Landing Ship, Tanks). They would land in amphibious tractors, and they made a practice run at the Tinian shore.

And so they left the Marianas on February 15, the LSTs going out first, and prepared to land on Iwo Jima on the morning of February 18, 1945.

The men were up at three o'clock in the morning, had their steak breakfast, and then got their gear ready for the landings. The men of the first ten waves of assault troops were aboard LSTs. The main body of the marines was aboard a number of transports, including one regiment of the Third Marine Division.

At dawn on February 18, the marines on the LSTs got the order to go below and board their assigned amphibious tractors. Down they went into the hold, where the tractors stood in two lines, facing the forward ramp. When the bow doors opened and the ramp was lowered they would go.

The marines climbed in and remained standing. They were crowded together with packs, gas masks, canteens, helmets, and an assortment of weapons and other equipment. The bow doors opened, the ramps went down, and the tractors began to move out. Soon five hundred tractors were bobbing around near the line of departure two miles offshore, where the command vessel would tell them when to go. At the line were Brigadier General Hart of the Fourth Marine Division and Brigadier General Leo Hermle of the Fifth Marine Division as observers.

First to go in would be sixty-eight amphibious tractors armed with 75mm guns. They did not carry any assault troops. Their task was to "swim" to shore, then climb the shore line to the first of the terraces that were the mark of Iwo Jima, establish themselves on the terraces, and protect the marines who followed them in the assault waves.

In one of the amphtracs a marine was singing an improvised song:

> "*Happy D Day to you.*
> *Happy D Day to you.*
> *Happy D Day dear marines,*
> *Happy D Day to you.*"

The weather, as Admiral Turner observed when he looked around at dawn, was ideal for a landing. The surf was down, the wind was almost nonexistent, the air was clear and fine, and the temperature was 70 degrees F.

The Japanese in their caves who looked out at the invasion fleet had a sinking feeling. It was so huge, so powerful, that it brought with it a feeling of doom to the defenders. And then, before the marines had begun assembling, the barrage had begun, and it continued as the little amphtracs bobbed around behind the line of departure.

The bombardment of D day would last five hours. First came the big guns of the battleships and cruisers supported by the destroyers, and then the wave of fighter planes and bombers, with the ships coming back again with more fire. And the assault landing craft would go in with their rockets, and the bombardment would then become a rolling action, moving up the hillsides as the troops came in, trying to pave the way for them.

At 8:15 the first three waves were ready at the line. At 8:30 the central control vessel dipped its pennant and the first wave started in those sixty-eight amphibious tractors of the Second Armored Amphibious Battalion, moving in as the naval shells whistled overhead. The mortar LVTs (Landing Vehicle, Tracked) units moved in for a last blast—20,000 rounds—at the beaches, and the second wave started off from the line, with nearly 1,500 marines in LVTs. Behind them were eight more waves, designed to land at five-minute intervals. When the leading wave was 400 yards offshore, the naval shelling stopped on schedule and the last air strike came in, low flying carrier planes that nearly scraped the beaches as they stormed across.

The first tractors with their 75mm guns hit the beach one minute early, at 8:59. In the next three minutes they were on the beaches: Beach Green, Beach Red One, Beaches Yellow One and Two, and Beach Blue One. Beach Blue Two turned out to be a boat basin.

Before the marines, rising sharply from the sea, was the first terrace. Ten feet of steep ground had to be covered to hit it, and when the first vehicles reached the shore, it was apparent that there was going to be a problem. For what looked like ordinary gray sand was volcanic ash and pebbles, much lighter than sand, and providing very little traction. When the tractors tried to go inland, they slipped and skidded in the gray mass. They shifted gears, and tried again. Some of them made it, grinding and sliding as they went. Some of them did not, and they slipped back into the sea and tried again, or stood off a little bit and blasted the shore with their 75mm guns. Down near Mt. Suribachi, at the southern end of the island, the going was worst, and virtually no amphtracs got ashore right away. Up north it was easier.

Mt. Suribachi's defense was entrusted to Colonel Kanehiko Atsuchi, who had about 2,000 men. The whole mountain was honeycombed with tunnels and caves, but the major element of the defense was at the base, in a belt of pillboxes and bunkers that were interconnected and ran back to caves in the mountain.

For the first few minutes, the Japanese seemed to be stunned by the invasion. There was no return fire, just the hammering of the ships offshore and the amphtracs as they came in. And when they hit the beach the men were out of the amphibious tractors and scrabbling for the first terrace. They found it very rough going: steep and slippery, and the weight of their equipment tended to bog them down. Some of the corpsmen carried more than fifty pounds, and a mortarman carried 122 pounds. It was rough, rough going.

The third wave hit the beach at 9:07, with 1,200 men. The fourth wave came in five minutes later, and another 1,600 marines were ashore.

No time was wasted. Colonel John Lanigan's Twenty-fifth Marines formed up and started off to the right, to move inland north toward the quarry. Colonel Walter Wensinger's Twenty-third moved straight toward Airfield No. 1. South of them, Colonel Thomas Wornham's Twenty-seventh Marines drove inland to hit the west coast and curve up around the airfield. Colonel Harry Liversedge's Twenty-eighth Marines would have the job of taking Mt. Suribachi, the extinct volcano at the southern end of the island whose steep slopes provided one of the key points of the Japanese defense, and from whose top one could see any point on the islands. The marines wanted that outpost, fast, for an observation post.

The Japanese were there in force, inside the mountain and on its slopes, with large concentrations of pillboxes and blockhouses and bunkers along the shore, put there to try to push the marines back into the sea before they could get established ashore. Nearest Mt. Suribachi was the 312th Japanese Independent Infantry Battalion. Behind Yellow Beach One was the Tenth Independent Anti-Tank Battalion. North of that unit, behind Yellow Beach Two, the 309th Independent Infantry waited. Each battalion numbered about 800 men.

For half an hour it seemed relatively easy. A few rounds of artillery burst near the shore. Some mortar rounds came in. But the enemy was not to be seen and hardly to be heard.

Lieutenant Wesley Bates was one of the first ashore. He scrambled up to the top of the terrace, and after the hard climb, lay there exhausted. It was so quiet he began to think that perhaps the Japanese had withdrawn from these positions and that it was going to be easy. He saw Sergeant Thorburn Thostensen and a marine corporal running to the first pillbox. They threw three grenades, and the corporal ran inside after the third one went off, his bayonet ready. He came out with the bayonet dripping blood, and trotted to the second pillbox. He jumped on top of it, and was cut down by fire from another pillbox.

So it was not going to be easy after all, Lieutenant Bates learned. The Japanese had carefully figured out the problems of firing, and one pillbox supported another, something the marines learned in a hurry. They started forward, leapfrogging, hitting some pillboxes that seemed easy, leaving others that seemed too dangerous.

In an hour it was getting hot, and the Japanese fire was getting hotter. One marine, running from one pillbox to another, had his pack literally shot off his back, and when he picked it up, the field jacket he had stuffed on top was nothing but a piece of bullet riddled rag.

Some marines were killed, some were wounded, some had narrow escapes, like Private First Class James Treadway, who

The Landings

was hit in the helmet by a bullet that cut across through the liner and left a bump on his head, and then went out the other side.

The first reports from the shore to the command ship *Eldorado* gave a very optimistic view to General Smith and Admiral Turner:

From the Twenty-fifth Regiment at the northern end of the beachhead: "Bogging down in heavy sand and steep terraces, but conditions generally favorable. Moving forward against airstrip under moderate fire."

From the Twenty-third Regiment in the center: "Four waves ashore and moving inland. Taking moderate mortar fire."

From the Twenty-seventh Marines, on the left of the Twenty-third: "Landings on schedule. Casualties unexpectedly light. Proceeding toward airstrip against light resistance."

From the Twenty-eighth Marines, moving toward Suribachi: "Troops ashore and moving to isolate volcano. Resistance moderate, but terrain awful."

Those reports were made just after nine o'clock.

An hour later, the tone had changed.

From the Twenty-fifth: "Catching all hell from the quarry. Heavy mortar and machine gun fire. Troops inland 200 yards but pinned down."

From the Twenty-third: "Taking heavy casualties and can't move for the moment. Mortars killing us."

From the Twenty-seventh: "All units pinned down by artillery and mortars. Casualties heavy. Need tank support to move anywhere."

From the Twenty-eighth: "Nearly across the neck, but taking heavy fire, and forward movement stopped. Machine gun and artillery fire heaviest ever seen."

The men of the First Battalion of the Twenty-eighth Marines pushed across the island. It was their job to get over to the west side as quickly as possible. They hurried, straight, and thus their left flank remained about 400 yards from Colonel Atsuchi's defense belt. But they were under fire from Suribachi's defenses nonetheless. The battalion attacked on a two-company front, with C Company on the right and B Company on the left. Soon shells were bursting up and down the line and small arms fire was coming in. Whole squads were pinned down by machine guns in pillboxes. Soon the two companies were strung out in battered columns. And the marines were learning one thing: Just knocking out the troops in a pillbox did not necessarily make that pillbox safe. The Japanese system of tunnels let them remain in a pillbox if it was not destroyed. As one marine said:

"When we secured a pillbox we would put up white flag to signify it had been taken care of. I looked into several of these and saw no sign of life. A little later these same pillboxes opened fire again. The Japanese could maneuver everywhere by means of underground passages."

And the Japanese very quickly showed a nasty pattern. They had their own trenches zeroed in for their guns, and as the day went along they also zeroed in the bomb craters and holes made by the 16-inch shells of the battleships. Every once in a while they would put some artillery fire into one of those holes or into a trench, and sometimes they hit one that was full of marines.

The First Battalion of the Twenty-eighth moved fast, but it took heavy casualties, particularly among the officers. Captain Phil Roach of C Company was hit in the knee. Captain Harold Rice was hit in the back of the neck.

But ninety minutes after the landing six men of Company B under Lieutenant Frank Wright and a few men from Company C reached the cliff overlooking the western beach.

But the fighting all the way was tough. Corporal Bill Faulkner was crossing one level area when he saw something that looked like a manhole cover up ahead. And underneath the hinged cover were a Japanese army helmet and two eyes. The lid dropped, and Faulkner squirmed his way up. The Japanese did not reappear, but Faulkner crawled around the area and found a sand mound and a tunnel entrance which he thought must be connected with the hinged, manhole cover of what was obviously a spider trap entrenchment with several openings. Corporal Conrad Shaker came up, and Faulkner suggested that they use grenades. But Shaker refused and drew his combat knife. All morning he had been using the knife to dispose of Japanese in the pillboxes and trenches. He slipped into the tunnel, was gone for a few minutes and returned with his pockets full of

The Landings 35

souvenirs and the knife bloody. Then he climbed up to a mound and shouted something to some marines behind him. As he did, a sniper shot him dead.

Faulkner went on forward. He came up to Sergeant Thostensen, who had also worked his way across the island. Thostensen was engaging in a rifle duel with a Japanese soldier who was inside the entrance to another tunnel. The sergeant would duck and a bullet would hiss by, and then he would return the fire. Finally he tossed a grenade into the tunnel and suddenly all was quiet. He explained to Faulkner then that he had a special grudge against that Japanese soldier. The first bullet in the shooting match had hit his pack and broken a bottle of Four Roses whiskey that he had carried carefully all the way across the island.

A Company, which had been held in reserve, arrived on the west side and took over a lot of the fighting. By noon, it was certain that the men who crossed were there to stay, although the fighting continued all the rest of the day.

The commander of the Second Battalion of the Twenty-eighth Marines was Lieutenant Colonel Chandler Johnson, a tough, little, fat man, who came charging off the beach that day, shouting "Okay, you bastards, let's get the hell off this beach," and who began the rush across the island to isolate Suribachi.

Back on the beach, as the Twenty-eighth Marines fought their way across the island and inland, life was growing much rougher as General Kuribayashi's men manned their artillery and mortars. A Fifth Division rocket section came out of the landing craft onto the beach, and artillery opened up on them. Three of the four rocket trucks were blasted out of commission, but the fourth got into action and its rockets hit an artillery dump on Mt. Suribachi, which went up with a great roar.

General Kuribayashi had told his men to be especially watchful for tanks, and when the tanks started coming ashore that morning they got much attention from the Japanese artillery. One marine watched as a tank started inland. It tried to edge over the first terrace and was hit by a mortar round that blew off the right tread. Marines began trying to get out of the turret.

Another mortar round lit right in the turret and all the marines inside were killed.

And when the tanks got up front, they were regarded by the marines as a mixed blessing, because they drew so much enemy fire.

By midmorning, conditions on the beach were becoming grim. Only high priority material was coming in at all: ammunition, communications equipment, rations, and medical supplies. Some of the amphtracs and amphibious trucks were taking their precious loads right up to the front lines, and they were always prime targets for shellfire and mortars.

On the beaches the Construction Battalions, the Seabees, were doing every sort of job, and stevedoring seemed to be one of the most important. The supplies had to be gotten off the beaches, and the wrecked vehicles were piling up. The Seabee caterpillar operators towed vehicles and dug revetments for the medics and supply dumps.

Shellfire was hellfire, as Lieutenant Benjamin Roselle, Jr., learned. At one o'clock in the afternoon he went ashore on the right side of the Fourth Division zone as leader of a naval gunfire liaison team. They were weighed down with radio gear, plodding inland. When they got about 200 yards inland, one man was killed by an artillery shell. Roselle picked up the man's gear and started forward again. Another round knocked three of them off their feet. Roselle's foot was badly wounded and he could not get up. The others bandaged his wound and stopped the flow of blood with a tourniquet. Several of his men had been wounded, and he ordered them to go back to the beach for evacuation.

Hell found the position: Two more men were killed, and Roselle was hit again in the other leg. Now only one man was left unwounded in the six-man team. They hugged the sand. The shellfire had a pattern, and after several rounds, another came in almost on top of them. Roselle was hit again in the shoulder, and the other man lost his right leg. The other man crawled away, and Roselle was left with the dead. And then another shell knocked him off the sand and wounded him in both thighs. He wondered what time it was and raised his hand to look at his watch. Another shell tore the watch from his wrist. Not long after this he was found by a team of medics, who got him to the beach and then to a hospital ship.

In the Twenty-third Marine sector, Captain LaVerne Wagner of the Third Battalion's Company K led his reserve company into the beach in the landing craft. The other companies of the Twenty-third that had made the assault were inland, and his job was to find them and relieve the outfit that needed it. This should have been easy in the beginning, requiring only that the company march in behind the others and take over up front. But the front was everywhere, as Wagner soon learned.

When his landing craft rammed into the beach, machine gunfire was slashing overhead. The men wanted to get out fast, but the ramp would not go down. Wagner ordered them over the side, and as one man rose he was hit in the face and shoulder by shrapnel. The rest dropped into waist-deep water, pushed up to the beach, and ran for shell holes. The beach was under mortar fire. It was crowded with wounded waiting to be evacuated. A few minutes after hitting the beach, Wagner's radioman lost his walkie-talkie, which was blown out of his hand. When the platoon had landed, Wagner started to move up toward the front. A machine gun found the company and men began to fall. Fifty yards inland, Lieutenant James Mariedas jumped into a shell hole to find that a Japanese was occupying it. They tussled, and the American managed to stab the Japanese to death with his own bayonet.

Ahead of Company K, the ground was studded with pillboxes. Some of them were still smoking from the effects of satchels full of explosives, and flamethrowers, but one erupted with machine gun fire. Captain Wagner called back for a tank, and one came up. But this was a really well-constructed pillbox, and the 75mm gun did not seem to make any impression on it. Other marines got around behind the pillbox and threw grenades in the back door. The grenades came flying out the front. Several men from K company circled the pillbox then and kept throwing the grenades through the apertures, until finally the pillbox was quiet. A marine went inside and found three dead

Japanese, with seventy-five unfired grenades all lined up on a shelf.

Company K moved up and found the assault troops, who were now dug in facing Airfield No. 1. As they came up they drew artillery fire and jumped for cover. They were pinned down by an antiaircraft gun that had been depressed to fire level. One squad tried its way around to the rear and found that the gun was operated by a single Japanese gunner. They shot him.

By this time Company K had taken thirty casualties, and was not yet in the front line. In fact, the company was still in reserve and had not been committed to "battle."

It was that way all across the island. There was no easy spot on Iwo that day. At the far end of the landing zone, up on Beach Blue, the Twenty-fifth Marines finally fought their way up the cliff, where they found and smashed several bunkers and also discovered several that had been smashed to pieces by direct hits from the navy gunfire. The casualties were very heavy, particularly in the Third Battalion, which lost nineteen of its officers.

That was the way it was going on Iwo Jima that first day.

CHAPTER SIX

Crossing the Island

Lieutenant Frank Wright's First Platoon of B Company reached the western shore of Iwo Jima at about 10:30 that morning. Wright had started out with sixty men, but by the time he got to the western side, only two of them were still with him. They had gone across, leapfrogging pillboxes and skirting bunkers. Private First Class Leo Zuck had gotten atop one 20mm gun pillbox and killed eight Japanese as they came out the back door. One, two, three, four, five, six, seven, eight!

The going was rough all the way. One marine had stuffed his field jacket into his pack, and on the way across machine gun fire had chewed up the pack and destroyed the field jacket. Another marine had real luck. A bullet came through his helmet and liner and went out the other side, just creasing his scalp.

Lieutenant Bates of C Company had recovered from his exhausting climb up to that first terrace and he also went across, arriving at about the same time as Lieutenant Wright. He had five men with him still. He turned back to look for his platoon sergeant. Everything seemed to be quiet. He had his rifle in his left hand and beckoned to a group of men with his right. They motioned back to him. Just then a machine gun opened fire and he was shot in the left forearm and fell. So that was what the others were trying to tell him!

Shocked for a few minutes thinking of the Purple Heart medal he had just won, he saw a corpsman running toward a marine who was bleeding from the head. He got up and called some men, who came to him, and soon he found out what had happened to his platoon. The platoon sergeant was wounded. The third squad leader was dead. His runner was wounded, and so were several of the other men. Some others were back there, not having gotten across yet.

Each marine had his own way of going. Captain Dwayne Mears was fighting his war this day with pistols. He was using a 45 caliber pistol to blow Japanese out of pillboxes, attacking one after the other. He got all the way to the west coast, and then he was hit by a bullet that pierced his throat with a mortal wound.

By the time the First Battalion of the Twenty-eighth Marines got across the island, there was only one company commander left in action, Captain Aaron G. Wilkins of A Company. He had kept the company down by the beach until the Second Battalion was ready to move toward Mt. Suribachi, which was its target. Then they started over.

Corporal Tony Stein went fast. He was a veteran of Guadalcanal, Vella LaVella, and Bougainville, and in the process of acquiring experience he had also acquired a weapon of his own manufacture. In civilian life he had been a toolmaker, so someplace along the line he had requisitioned a 30 caliber machine gun from the wreckage of a navy fighter, and had fashioned it into a handheld machine pistol. He called his weapon "the stinger" and it was so effective he was knocking off pillboxes, one after the other, along with Sergeant Merritt Savage and Corporal Frederick Tabert. Stein went in first, his "stinger" spitting fire, and then Sergeant Savage came up with a charge and blew the pillbox, while Corporal Tabert covered them. In the first hour of the crossing Stein killed twenty Japanese. He would run out of ammunition and then go back down to the beach and get more, and start the process again. Eight times he went back for ammunition that day. Twice his "stinger" was shot out of his hand, but each time he recovered it and went after the Japanese again.

After about two hours the First Battalion of the Twenty-eighth Marines was across the island in force, and Company

E came up to begin to move into the scrubwood, where they knew the Japanese had strong positions. Corporal Richard Wheeler and Marine Private Howard Snyder were moving along abreast when they got near the scrub, and suddenly a machine gun began to fire on them. The bullets ricocheted around their feet. They jumped into a shallow depression, and immediately realized that this was not the right place to be. They were exposed to the machine gun on the side, and bursts splashed sand into their faces. They scrambled out of there and Wheeler found a shell hole. It was much too shallow for good cover but better than nothing. He bent very low to keep down. The platoon commander, Lieutenant Wells, who was in another shell hole, said he was going to leave his pack and gas mask, and come back for them later. That would make it a lot easier to move fast, because it would strip at least twenty pounds of weight away. Wheeler did the same. But he couldn't get his pack off in his shell hole, and he ended up cutting the straps with his combat knife. Wheeler still had plenty of weight to carry: a helmet and liner, rifle, bayonet, three grenades, cartridge belt full of cartridges, knife, two canteens and a first aid kit. These made up about twenty-five pounds.

When they were ready to go, Lieutenant Wells stood up, and so did the others. They had expected to be greeted by machine gun fire, but the gun had closed down again (following General Kuribayashi's instructions) and the area was silent for the moment. They moved along through grassy hummocks, toward the scrub. They passed a wounded marine, lying with his head on his folded poncho, his shirt open and a bloody bandage on his midriff.

"Hey Mac," the wounded man shouted, "do you know if there's a stretcher coming for me?"

"Yeah, I think so," said Wheeler. He hadn't seen an aid man since the beach, but it was either lie or get involved and maybe have to go back down to the beach and find some stretcher bearers. Too soon they were out in the open and fast approaching the scrub brush. Dead ahead they saw a mound of sand, and beneath the top of the mound an ominous rectangular opening, a pillbox, reinforced concrete under the sand. It could be big enough for a machine gun or a mortar. Whatever it was, it meant trouble if there was anyone in there. But that was what they didn't know. Maybe somebody had already taken care of it. Maybe the Japanese had abandoned it.

But then they had their answer. The black aperture suddenly turned orange and machine gun bullets came spitting out. The marines jumped for cover, some of them finding shell holes and some falling behind a terrace about a foot high that extended across their path. Nobody was hit, but Lieutenant Wells made a jump for a shell hole and landed squarely on top of a dead Japanese soldier who had been killed by the naval bombardment. The body was lying on its back with its viscera hanging out, and Wells landed on his knees on top of the body. At that moment it didn't seem important.

The cover was anything but complete, and they all felt exposed. They pressed flat against the ground. They were in the classic position, pinned down by a machine gun.

The book had the answer and they had done it dozens of times in training. One man would start forward with a demolition charge in a wide circle. All the others would cover him with all the fire they could muster, as he crawled up to the pillbox. Then he would dash forward the last few yards, stuff the charge into the gun aperture, and run like hell to get out of there. The riflemen would stop firing while he was doing his last bit of the act, and then pour it on again even harder if they could to keep the Japanese from pushing the charge out of the pillbox. The charge would go off, and presto, no more pillbox and a handful of dead Japanese in the wreckage.

That was the way it was supposed to work. The catch was that somebody had to take that satchel charge up to the pillbox. And who was it going to be? That was Lieutenant Wells's business.

Everybody was waiting, when suddenly they heard a shell explode about fifty yards to the right. They looked, and another shell raised a jet of sand. Somebody was shooting with a field piece, and he seemed to be moving toward them. But then they saw what the gun was shooting at: a pair of beautiful olive green Sherman tanks which had come up from the east beach, and made it across the island. Four of the tanks had been knocked

Crossing the Island 43

out before they got across, but the others were coming. And here were two of them. They headed straight for the pillbox with their 75mm guns firing. They got into pointblank range and stopped and continued to fire until they had knocked out the pillbox and all was quiet inside. A fortress had become a tomb.

Lieutenant Wells and his men got up and began to move again. They reached the fringe of the scrub brush and there they ran into a whole network of Japanese trenches—empty trenches and antitank ditches. Captain Osada's 312th Independent Infantry Battalion had been here in strength in the early morning, 800 men strong, but if half that number had survived the shelling, it was a miracle. The rolling barrage had struck his outfit and the 309th Infantry Battalion up by Beach Yellow One. In one platoon only ten of forty men had survived the shelling and they had scattered.

So far, E ("Easy") Company had been lucky. Corporal Wheeler's platoon had lost only two men, who had been hit on the beach. They had covered 500 yards to cross the island without taking another casualty.

Now the men fell into single file, and Lieutenant Wells led them along the trenches and antitank ditches in the direction they wanted to go, to the western shore. It was another 400-yard trip. The going was slow. The men stopped, and Wells went forward with a man or two to reconnoiter, and then came back and got them.

They moved through pillboxes and bunkers, some of them shot up and some of them intact. They had no way of knowing if those whole pillboxes and bunkers held live Japanese or not, and it was not their business to stop and find out if they were not bothered. That was to be left to the men of the Fifth Engineer Battalion, who would be coming along with the material to do it. Some of the bunkers looked like igloos, and some like sandpiles. One of them sounded like the Fourth of July, with machine gun or rifle ammunition popping off inside. It had obviously been taken care of by somebody up ahead.

Now the men of Easy Company began to encounter the casualties of the early assault companies. Little knots of wounded men were lying on the sand and grass in the antitank ditches, waiting for evacuation. Some of them looked up as the marines passed, but nobody said anything.

They thought it strange that they did not see many Japanese dead. A few here and there, lying half in and half out of a pillbox. But not many. General Kuribayashi's orders were to recover casualties, and prevent the enemy from learning how many they had imposed.

The men of Company E were moving through a trench waist deep, with an antitank ditch running alongside about fifty feet to the right, when suddenly they heard the sound of rapid Japanese voices. An officer motioned them to get down, and they dropped. The voices continued for a moment, a jumble of noise, and then they began to diminish. Soon they had stopped. The Japanese had gone.

Lieutenant Wells got up and began moving ahead again. Moving into a shallow declivity between two sand ridges, he was looking at a battered fuselage of a Japanese airplane when he almost tripped over a land mine that was sticking out of the sand. Carefully he put his foot down elsewhere, and stepped around the mine, then detailed a man to stand by it and keep anybody else from getting hit.

They continued to move slowly. It was late afternoon when they approached the defense perimeter of the First Battalion, set up by the early arrivals along the high ground overlooking the western beach of Iwo Jima. They found their place and began to set up, keeping an eye on the several pillboxes and bunkers nearby.

At the base of one mound which had not been touched lay two badly wounded marines who would die in the next few hours. An officer was sitting next to them. Lieutenant Wells took a look at the mound. He did not like its looks. It was big enough to hold a field piece, and if it was full of Japanese . . .

He asked the lieutenant with the wounded men to get them out of there so he could blow the bunker. The lieutenant did not want to move the men, but Wells insisted that it was a danger to the perimeter, and the lieutenant finally gave in. Just as the men were being carried away, a captain of the First Battalion came up and looked at the untouched bunker.

"That's just a supply dump," he said. "I've been around here all afternoon. There's nobody in there. There's no use wasting a charge on that."

So Lieutenant Wells was overruled and outranked, and he backed off and went about the business of establishing the platoon perimeter for the night.

As soon as the men got the perimeter established, Wells took them into the scrub brush, to which they had not paid much attention so far, just to see that there were not any Japanese in there. He went forward with a Thompson submachine gun and a marine with a Garand and bayonet. They were kicking around the scrub and making some commotion, when suddenly the concrete door on the right side of the "supply dump" rolled open and out came a 3-inch field piece spitting shells along the perimeter to the southwest.

Wells was about to order an attack on the bunker when a lieutenant from another First Battalion platoon came up with several men screened by the bushes. Then the bunker began to spout machine gun fire. A marine rushed the bunker with a shaped charge, scratched the top sand of the bunker away, set the charge, and dashed off. The charge blew, and the Japanese inside hastily closed the apertures to their bunker. Another marine now came up with a thermite grenade and tossed it in the hole in the top of the bunker. It went off and white smoke began to come out. The concrete door on E Company's side of the bunker burst open and a wave of smoke rushed out. Feet could be seen in green sneakers in the smoke-filled bunker. Wells and the other marine began firing their weapons into the bunker. Wells fired a whole forty-round clip of the Thompson and the marine fired all eight rounds of his Garand. Three men stumbled out of the bunker and fell. One tried to get up, and the marine bayoneted him until he was still.

Then a grenade came out of a thicket several yards to the left and Lieutenant Wells yelled. The marine dropped flat and the fragments slashed the air over him. He was not hit. Lieutenant Wells put a fresh drum in the Thompson submachine gun and ran toward the thicket to get the grenade thrower. He kept a low profile; it was growing dark and he wanted to see the silhouette of the Japanese against the sky. But he found nothing. The Japanese had fled.

CHAPTER SEVEN

The Airfield

Colonel Thomas Wornham's Twenty-seventh Marines were given the job of driving inland to curve around west of Airfield No. 1, while Colonel Walter Wensinger's Twenty-third Marines moved straight inland toward the airfield. On Beach Red One, Company E and Company F of the Twenty-seventh's Second Battalion landed in the first waves, while the First Battalion landed on Beach Red Two. In the confusion of landing, the companies got mixed up, and Company A and Company B changed places in relation to Company C. But they were ashore at last, and ready to start moving quickly across the southern end of Airfield No. 1. Colonel Wornham and his staff came in on an LVT.

"All right," shouted the colonel, as the ramp of the LVT ground down on the bottom, "be ready to bail out of here goddam fast!"

When the landing ramp hit, he was one of the first out. Behind him the marines tried to run, but the gray sand came up over the tops of their combat boots and tripped them up. They could slog along; they could not run. The beach was lined with the trenches that had been dug by the Japanese, and deserted in the bombardment of the morning—three trench lines in the first thirty yards from shore. Now those trenches were full of American marines lying panting after the hard push up the hill, panting and listening to the sounds of the mortar shells dropping around them.

Some of the marines were pinned down in this trench line

for forty minutes. Eventually they had to move and they did, upward and forward.

War correspondent John Lardner was moving ahead and stopped at one of the dunes for a blow. Something moved beside the next dune. It was a wounded marine, who had been hit by shrapnel in the arm, the leg, buttocks, and eye. He was most worried about his eye. Lardner had to go close to him so the man could hear, because he had been deafened by the explosion that had wounded him. He wanted to know if there were corpsmen around. There weren't any. Enemy fire on the beach was making it hard for the corpsmen to work. Lardner promised to look for a corpsman and to report on this marine as soon as possible, and went on.

Soon he came to a Japanese pillbox where a marine was sitting. The pillbox had walls three feet thick, and was built on a frame of metal tubing.

One machine gun platoon of the First Battalion was led by Sergeant John Basilione, known to the platoon as Manila John. He already held the Medal of Honor, which he had won on Guadalcanal by holding off a Japanese assault singlehandedly with two machine guns and a pistol. Now he was running for the west coast of Iwo Jima, with his men behind him. It was 10:30 in the morning and the Japanese were fully aroused and ready to fight in their own way, in order to cause the most attrition to the marines. Bring out the weapons only when there is something to shoot at, they were told. Manila John and his men were something to shoot at, and a mortar on the hills opened up on them. A shell burst, and five men were suddenly dead, among them Manila John.

But the others of the Twenty-seventh Marines went on, and turned north beyond the airfield. They ran into Major Tatsumi's 311th Independent Infantry Battalion, or what was left of it. The heavy early Japanese casualties were almost all taken by the troops who had responded to the navy's demand for defense at the water's edge. Before the end of this one day, the 311th would suffer 50 percent casualties in its roster of 700 men.

But the marines were taking heavy casualties. Lutheran Chaplain Louis Valbracht went in on one of the early boats. As

The Airfield 49

he ran for the first terrace, he encountered a marine limping back to the shore, one foot bare and bleeding. Shrapnel had torn off his shoe and several toes. "Short war," said the wounded marine to the chaplain as they passed, and then he limped on, toward the beach and the ride to the hospital ship and probably home. He was one of the lucky ones. The chaplain hurried across the rough terrain, bound for the west side. Halfway across he sank down to rest at a shattered Japanese pillbox. His eye fell on a foot, a bare foot, a white foot. Just a foot. He turned his head to the right. Twenty yards away in a shell hole lay the mangled remains of four marines. One of them was missing a foot.

Colonel Wornham had reached a little plateau above the beach, and there, in a big shell hole created for him by one of the battleships, he had set up his command post. Now he was worried about communication with his battalions. Such problems as the confusion of Companies A, B, and C of the First Battalion, with B Company being where A company should be in relation to C Company, could create a lot of confusion.

The colonel was surrounded by staff men, messengers, and radio operators, and he was following by radio and by messenger the progress of his three battalions. It was organized confusion now, with men coming and going and hanging around the radios to find out what was going on with the battalions.

Aboard the ships it was the same. Men gathered around any radio they could find and tried to follow the progress of the battle ashore. A marine sitting in a jeep on the deck of one of the transports sounded like a broadcaster at a football game.

"We're in a hundred yards," he called out, and the sailors around him cheered.

"The tanks are up another hundred yards." They cheered again.

In the radio rooms of the warships the men on watch got specific information.

"Naval gunfire in Target Area 181, please" came a call from an aerial observer aloft in one of the planes.

"Air observer Fourth Division reports enemy gun and mortar positions in TA 16 6 CD." [That was the quarry, one of the really rough Japanese strongholds.]

50 IWO JIMA

"Mission 11 enemy gun positions in TA 183 1 W.Q.D. will be attacked by bombs, rockets, and machine gun fire as soon as possible. Three oh five Lucky [a sixteen-plane squadron] will expend all ammunition on this attack."

Those listening on the aerial observer circuit heard the cross talk.

"Air observer Fifth Division reports six friendly tanks on southern end of Airfield No 1. Have stopped."

"Three torpedo planes with propaganda leaflets are now orbiting Point Sugar awaiting instructions."

And they heard Major Ray Dollings, spotting for the Fifth Division, singing a parody of one of the hit tunes from the Broadway show *Oklahoma:*

"Oh what a beautiful morning
Oh what a beautiful day.
I've got a terrible feeling
Everything's coming my way."

And it did. The Japanese antiaircraft batteries began firing the plane in which the major was riding was hit, bucked, and began spiralling down into the sea, to crash in the water near a group of assault craft moving in to shore. One of the boat rushed over to the crashed plane, and picked up two bodies, the pilot and the major.

In a little while it was apparent that the Fourth Marine Division on the northeastern beaches was getting the brunt of the Japanese defense. Colonel Walter Wensinger's Twenty-third Marines landed on Beach Yellow One and Beach Yellow Two Colonel John Lanigan's Twenty-fifth Marines landed on Beach Blue One. This was in the heart of General Kuribayashi's static defense system, with its interconnecting maze of tunnels, caves and underground caverns, five and six stories deep. On the high ground north of the beaches, the Japanese had a system of observation posts. They had planned the fields of fire for their weapons months earlier, and now they waited.

They waited through the three days of bombardment, and the D Day bombing bombardment and rocketing by ships and planes. Deep inside the mountain that was Iwo Jima they waited in their caves and tunnels, and when the naval gunfire lifted, they came out and brought their weapons up to the surface.

Still the Japanese waited.

The first wave of the Twenty-third Marines hit the beach. Nothing happened. One marine who had been at Tarawa and remembered the hail of fire they walked into that day in 1942 found it hard to understand.

"There's something screwy here," he said. The First Battalion of the Twenty-third hit Yellow One and moved across. No enemy fire. The Second Battalion hit Yellow Two and began to move, slowly because of the lava sand, but steadily and without opposition. It all seemed so easy. For a few minutes it *was* easy, and then the Japanese came to life.

Guns and mortars on the heights began to fire. Four Landing Ships Medium, carrying tanks, were hit by mortar shells as they pulled up to the beach, and suffered extensive damage.

As the aerial observers called for fire, they began to learn something about those defenses. They got the fire—from the battleships, cruisers and destroyers—but all too often, it did nothing to help the marine infantry on the beach and struggling to get up the incline to the airfields. It took a direct hit to knock out a gun emplacement. And soon they found that some of the installations could even stand a direct hit. They were built underground, with only a firing slit uncovered, and the whole installation was concealed by an artificial sandbank or rock pile It was very difficult to spot these guns unless they were actually firing. Even the gunports for the mortars were only a foot or two wide.

Fire came from the front and from the flanks, from pillboxes, bunkers, and blockhouses, from ditches, and apparently from nowhere.

Directly in front of the Twenty-third Marines stood two huge blockhouses and fifty pillboxes. These were a part of the naval insistence on defense at the water's edge, reminiscent of Tarawa, and the blockhouses had been hit repeatedly by naval shellfire and bombs and rockets, and were partly destroyed. But inside there were still Japanese and there were still mortars and machine guns—and they were firing on the beaches.

Enemy fire was not the only problem. The calm of morning that had so impressed Admiral Turner did not last. The surf began to come up, and by nine o'clock the beaches were clogging up with LVTs that were damaged by enemy fire or bogged down. The LCVP (Landing Craft, Vehicles and Personnel) came in when these light boats hit the beach, the surf smashed them and many of them were broached. Some were swamped, and these and boats that were hit by gunfire piled in behind and stuck on the beach. If the traffic kept going this way, soon the beaches would be impassable.

It soon became apparent that the key to the success of the landings on the upper east side lay in the quarry and north of it, from where the most murderous fire was coming. The First Battalion of the Twenty-fifth Marines landed on Blue One. Lieutenant Colonel Hollis Mustain saw that his men had to go up around the airfield and get to the top of the quarry. The heights must be taken to stop the fire against the beaches.

Company A came in on the third wave, to Yellow One. Almost immediately, the company radioman was hit, and Captain John Kalen crawled to him to give him a hand. The captain was hit too, and the hail of fire that came down on the beach kept the others from moving to help. They watched without being able to move as the captain bled to death from his wounds.

With Captain Kalen down, First Lieutenant William Worsham assumed command of the company. He got the second platoon off the beach, and two hundred and fifty yards inland. There they were stopped by interlocking machine gun fire from pillboxes. The third platoon was stuck a hundred yards behind.

The commander of the Twenty-third's First Battalion called for artillery support and tanks. But the infantrymen didn't wait. Sergeant Darrell Cole took his machine gun squad up against the lines of pillboxes, one after another, firing into the apertures as they came up to the pillboxes, tossing grenades and moving on. When the machine gun jammed, he threw more grenades. He went back twice to the beach to get more grenades. He used them up and went back for a third load. This time, a Japanese grenade exploded at his feet and killed him. But because of Cole's ferocity, most of the men of his platoon got off that beach alive.

At one o'clock in the afternoon, the situation ashore was extremely confused. Landing craft were wrecking and piling up on the beaches. Two miles out at sea, boats circled the command boat and waited for a signal to head to shore with reinforcements, ammunition, tanks, trucks, bulldozers, fuel, and water. But the beachhead was so cluttered that shortly after one P.M. Admiral Turner closed the beaches until enemy fire slackened and something could be done to clear up the confusion. Nothing moved toward the shore for nearly two hours. Finally at almost three o'clock some tanks began to land, along with the first of the reserves, the Twenty-sixth Marines. They moved into heavy fire and the wreckage, and it took nearly two hours to get them off the beach. Before they reached the slope, they had suffered heavy casualties.

The last of the Fifth Division troops to land were the men of the Third Battalion of the Twenty-seventh Marines, who had gotten into their landing craft at nine o'clock in the morning. They did not get to shore for seven hours. They moved into confusion: wounded men, men waiting to be evacuated, wrecked amphtracs, and heavy shelling. But by twilight they were on the edge of the airstrip and digging in.

Lieutenant Worsham decided to move around Company B to get his men out of the field of fire from the pillboxes. He was killed. First Lieutenant Frank Devoe, commander of the mortar platoon, took over. Almost immediately he was wounded in the shoulder, but he kept on going. Then First Lieutenant Arthur Zimmerman led the men of Company A around Company B and toward the airfield. The company came to a blockhouse and was stopped by the intense fire. All along the line on the Yellow beaches came the call for tank support. The LSMs were called to come in, and three of them hit the Yellow beaches, landing sixteen Sherman tanks. They began to make a difference.

Lieutenant Zimmerman went back to find a tank, and brought it up to the position. The Sherman's 75mm gun began firing and the blockhouse went silent. The men of Company A hurried up with demolition charges, blew up the blockhouse, and moved on. All afternoon they moved ahead with agonizing slowness. By dusk they were near the airfield and stopped for rest.

Lieutenant Zimmerman was looking for Lieutenant Worsham, whom he thought was still in command of the company. Devoe came up to him out of nowhere, his left arm dangling.

"You've been in command of the company for the last two hours," he told Zimmerman. And then he headed down for the beach and a boat back to the fleet. Zimmerman, the fourth commander of Company A of the day, set about preparing the perimeter for the night.

CHAPTER EIGHT

The Twenty-Fifth Marines Had a Little Problem . . .

The Yellow and Red Beaches were the bad ones, and if anyone had to pick the worst, probably Beach Red One would have won the honor hands down. Robert Sherrod, the *Time-Life* correspondent, came into that beach a little after the first few waves, and saw bodies, bodies, bodies. Many of them were cut in half, and legs and arms lay strewn away from the trunks. In one spot he saw a string of human guts fifteen feet long spilled out on the sand. Just guts. No bodies. And there was meat: unidentifiable meat, red and pink and grisly. Just meat. The blood had been washed away by the surf. This was the sort of carnage that General Kuribayashi's men were able to wreak with their carefully planned fields of fire and their patient waiting.

Sergeant T. Grady Gallant, a squad leader of the Twenty-fifth Marines, went in with the third wave. Their platoon had a 37mm antitank gun to support the advance. The question was, where to put it. Sergeant Gallant went ashore to find out, while the gun was being horsed off a landing craft.

He and another marine scrambled up the bank to the first terrace. They saw nothing there. They looked back. Scattered along the beach southward, they saw wrecked amphtracs, some of them still smoking, some of them with big pieces gone, others flooded out and listing, with the surf breaking over them. The marines were too far away to see all the bullet holes. They didn't see any people. Where were the first two waves? They had to be somewhere up ahead. But they were out of sight from the terrace. All the sergeant could see was rock and the sea and the beach and the wreckage.

Even the bodies on the beach from this distance melded into the beach itself and were just a part of the scene.

Back of the surf line, clusters of little boats milled around, some of them heading in, but most heading out to sea. Some were adrift and wallowing, dead in the water with men bailing furiously with helmets to keep them afloat. A battleship stood close in to the shore, its bow pointed toward Mt. Suribachi, its guns depressed to aim at the coastal artillery that had already made itself known on the mountain. Smoke drifted away from the side of the mountain—smoke from incoming fire of the battleship and other ships, and smoke and red flashes of fire from the Japanese guns.

The sergeant looked toward the cliff ahead of them, the rock rising sharply ahead. Iwo Jima. It was anything but a beauty spot: No trees, no grass, just gray bleak rock and lava dust. From the flat beach the ground rose sharply to that first terrace and then to the next, but it was rock, all rock, and underneath that rock there had to be a maze of Japanese defenses, not one of which they could see.

Down on the beach nothing was moving. There were marines along that beach and ahead of them—that they knew, but they could not see them. Nor could they see any sign of the enemy except for the occasional flashes from the mountainside that gave away for just a moment the position of an enemy weapon.

They moved to the top of the bank and were on the next terrace. They looked around. There was nothing. No movement, no people. The surface was pockmarked with shell holes and bomb craters from the pasting the island had been taking for many days, weeks, and months, if one counted the efforts of the carrier planes, B-24s and B-29s which had all hit the island time and again. The sergeant and the other marine studied the terrace and tried to make up their minds whether they should cross it

The Twenty-Fifth Marines Had a Problem... 57

not. What was out there? What was under there? What would happen if they ventured out there?

They decided to dig in, just in case someone started firing mortars at them. They started to dig with their hands in the loose gravel. It came up like marbles, but as fast as they dug the loose gravel, it poured back into the holes. There was no way to dig a foxhole here and have it stay. They quit trying. They crawled up to the top of the next bank and ran across the terrace. It was just like the one they had just left, flat and empty, about twenty feet wide, and at the end of it was another sloping bank and up above that another terrace that went a little farther inland.

Off to the right they saw marines. They recognized the color of the clothes. They were lying at the base of the bank. They seemed to be waiting for something. Maybe they were under mortar fire. The sergeant could not tell from here. He and the other marine decided to go over to the marines and find out what they knew. They dashed across the terrace and hit the third bank, to join the other marines. Nobody moved as they came up.

Then it came to them.

All these dozen men lying there against the bank were dead.

They looked at the bodies. Each of them was the same, with small holes stitched along the back. They had been killed by automatic weapons fire, and it was not hard to figure out how. The Japanese had lain doggo, to let this line of marines come up and go past. Then they had emerged from whatever warren they were now in and, automatic weapons blazing, they had shot the whole squad down, in the back. Every man had died in position, without time to move or turn or run. They lay there against the bank, faces in the dirt, dead.

It occurred to the sergeant and the other marine simultaneously: What happened to those men might be about to happen to them, too. They turned and ran as fast as they could, stumbling through the gravel and the dust, until they were back at what now seemed to be that friendly first bank where they had started.

Sergeant Gallant and the other marine moved off the bank then and down to the beach, and headed south toward Mt. Suribachi, following the base of the bank that gave them protection from the inland side of the island where they knew the Japanese were. They were still looking for someone to tell them what was going on. Each carried a 30 caliber carbine in his hands.

After they had gone about fifty yards, they turned up the bank and climbed. Ahead of them they saw a big hole made by a bomb or by a 16-inch shell. They dashed up and dropped into it, spraying gravel as they slid down the inside. There on the opposite side sat two marines, knees drawn up under their chins, cradling their M-1 rifles with the bayonets on the end. The two marines seemed only mildly interested in the new arrivals.

"What's the situation?" Sergeant Gallant asked one of the marines.

"We don't know," said the marine. "It's a mess."

They all agreed on that. They sat and smoked cigarettes in companionable silence. Occasionally they could hear a mortar round land somewhere. Occasionally a bullet whisked by, but only occasionally. From the sound they all knew these bullets and mortar rounds were not meant for them.

A corpsman appeared on the lip of the shell hole. As he stepped to the edge, gravel poured down into the shell hole.

The corpsman wanted some help. He had three men to carry a stretcher. A photographer just over the hill had been "shot up pretty bad," and had to be gotten to the beach. It wouldn't take long.

The four marines sitting in the shell hole debated the issue. To go or not to go? No one wanted to volunteer. Volunteering just got you into trouble, they all agreed.

They decided the photographer was nuts, out taking pictures even before the beach was secure. No wonder he had got shot up.

The sergeant took the photographer's side. He had been taking pictures because the brass wanted to see what was going on.

Then the brass ought to come to the beach and see, said the others.

In the end, one of the two marines on the far side of the shell hole ended up going. He climbed up the side of the shell hole

The Twenty-Fifth Marines Had a Problem . . . 59

loosing a new fury of gravel, and disappeared over the rim.

The sergeant and the other two marines remained, debating the issues of helping people and volunteering, either of which might result in trouble and maybe even get a man killed.

Sergeant Gallant and his companion finally left the shelter of the shell hole and got back to their business. They went down to the beach to start over again. Their expedition had come to nothing, except to find twelve men dead, ambushed by the Japanese, and to get involved in a rescue party.

Down on the beach the two marines came to an impromptu aid station where a dozen stretchers were gathered, with wounded marines waiting for a LST to come and take them to a hospital ship.

They met another marine there, a marine with whom they had ridden in to the landing. That gave them a sort of kinship, and the other marine told them something they did not know. They had also come in with a doctor, a sort of a philosophical doctor, who had told them that the Japanese were not bad people, just misled by the militarists. They had listened to him and he had seemed to make some sense. Not that it mattered now, because the other marine told them that their doctor friend was dead. He had been hit by a shell a few minutes after landing. Not a mortar round, but an artillery shell from the mountain. The shell had blown off the doctor's legs below the knee and hit him in the guts. He had died quickly and never knew he did not have any legs any more.

For a few minutes the sergeant listened to this tale and thought about the doctor. On the way in, the doctor had told them about his wedding, and the fact that he had only a seventy-two hour pass for a honeymoon, and how his wife was a nurse, working in a hospital in the States and waiting for him to come home. And now he wouldn't be going home. Just like a lot of other guys on this beach.

After a while, Sergeant Gallant broke it off. There were too many people on that little bit of beach and the Japanese might get it in their heads to start shooting again. They went back to their original spot on the bank, crawled to the top, and noticed that the fire now was much heavier on the terrace than it had been earlier.

Sergeant Gallant was feeling frustrated. Here he was on Iwo Jima, and the marines had a strip of island less than twenty feet wide under control. It was a helluva note, he thought. The enemy was firing on them from two flanks, from the front and from above.

The Japanese saw the little clot of men on the beach down below and, obeying General Kurabayashi's instructions to reduce the enemy whenever there was something at which to fire, began firing again. Their shells fell among the stretchers and either wounded the wounded again or killed them. One man sat upright on his stretcher and started to scream. He screamed for minutes, filling the air with his screams, so loud that they rent the ears of the sergeant on the terrace above the beach. And the sergeant wished that the wounded man would lie down and die. Eventually the screaming stopped. The man did die. Then the silence was as disturbing as the screaming had been.

Sergeant Gallant and the marine with him went back to the point where they had entered this terrifying picture—back to the beach.

There, 50 feet from the shore, stood the instrument that had sent them on the chase up and over the terraces, to find the twelve dead marines, to come back and witness the killing of the wounded marines on their stretchers.

There stood the 37mm antitank gun. The waves of the surf were breaking over its muzzle and its wheels were deeply embedded in the sand.

Eight marines were gathered around the gun, cursing and pulling on the trail and trying to move the embedded wheels against the push of water and the pull of sand. The men pushed and cursed and hauled and fell into the surf and got up and pushed and pulled again. Inch by inch, they pulled the gun in to the shore.

It was now a few minutes before eleven o'clock in the morning on February 19, 1945. The battle of Iwo Jima had been in progress for—how long? For not quite two hours, if you were a marine on the shore. For three and a half days, if you were a

The Twenty-Fifth Marines Had a Problem . . .

sailor on one of the ships involved in the artillery barrage. Here and there for a few hours, if you were a carrier pilot who came, bombed and strafed, and left. For four and a half months, if you were a Japanese soldier who had lived through the almost daily bombing and strafing and naval bombardments conducted by the Americans.

Now everything revolved around that 37mm antitank gun and what was to be done with it.

When the eight marines got the gun to the shore and collapsed against the bank, panting, the beach was almost quiet. Down below them back at the scene of the aid station carnage they could see corpsmen sorting out stretchers, and did not know why this was being done. Sergeant Gallant knew. The corpsmen were separating the wounded from the new dead, those who had not lived through the shelling of the enclave of the wounded.

An occasional landing craft arrived, bearing a messenger or a specialist or some special equipment. But they were few, very few. For the moment the beach was virtually deserted.

The battalion commander, a lieutenant colonel, appeared on the beach, smoking a cigarette and armed with a 45 caliber Colt automatic pistol. A second lieutenant came up and the lieutenant colonel told him to get the gun up on the terrace and lay some fire against the cliff above.

Where did the lieutenant colonel want the fire? "Any particular place?" asked the lieutenant.

He looked up at the cliff. There was nothing to look at but cliff.

"No," said the lieutenant colonel. "No particular place. Just fire at the cliff. The Japs are there."

The lieutenant motioned to a platoon sergeant. When he came over, the lieutenant told him to move the gun to the first terrace and lay down some fire on the cliff.

"Any particular place?" asked the platoon sergeant.

"No," the lieutenant said. "Just shoot at the cliff. The Japs are up there."

The platoon sergeant went to the bank where the eight men who had lugged the gun out of the surf were sitting. He told them to take the gun to the first terrace and open fire on the cliff.

The buck sergeant in charge of the detail looked at the cliff.

"Any special target?"

"No," said the platoon sergeant. "Just shoot."

The buck sergeant observed that it might be better to have a target to shoot at.

"Have you seen anything to shoot at?" asked the platoon sergeant.

"No," said the buck sergeant.

"That's right," said the platoon sergeant. "Then just shoot."

Nobody knew where the Japanese were. They were covered up and nobody knew where to shoot.

The buck sergeant told his eight men to get the gun up onto the terrace. The eight marines looked at the terrace and they looked at the gun. Two marines picked up the trail. The other six gathered around, finding handholds on the shield and the muzzle.

"It'll have to go up trail first," said the buck sergeant.

The marines swung the trail around, so it pointed at the bank. The buck sergeant grasped the ring on the end of the trail and pulled. The marines on the trail pulled; the others pushed. They got the wheels to the bank. They hit the bank, and the wheels and their feet sank into the gravel. The trail went up. The muzzle went down and hit the sand of the beach. The gun was stuck. It would not move.

Try as they might, they could not budge the gun.

An amphibious tractor came along, having unloaded on the beach and ready to go back to the ship. The marines stopped the tractor driver and asked for a hand with the gun. The noise of the tractor engine was so loud that the driver and the sergeant had to shout at each other, but the sergeant got through. Sure, said the driver, he would give them a hand. "Where to?"

"Up on the terrace," said the buck sergeant.

They hooked the trail of the 37mm gun to the amphtrac and the driver gunned the engine.

It was easy. The tractor went up the bank and the gun went along behind. In a minute it was done. The gun was safely up on the terrace.

The Twenty-Fifth Marines Had a Problem . . . 63

The marines climbed up and unhooked the gun. The amphtrac driver then looked around for the best way to turn around and get back to sea. He saw a narrow dirt road ahead and headed into that. It widened up ahead. There was plenty of room to turn around.

The marines watched as he maneuvered.

The driver turned the amphtrac into the road and to the wide place and swung around.

As he turned, a thunderous explosion shook the air, and smoke and flame gushed out from beneath the tractor. The fuel tank exploded and the tractor rose six feet in the air and then fell back, flames swirling around it. But the driver kept going up. His body rose, turning, his arms straight out, his legs apart, and the body went up, up, up.

"He hit a mine," said one marine.

"That must of been one helluva mine," said another.

"Look at him, look at him!"

They all looked. The tractor driver's body was high in the air and still going up.

"It must be up seventy-five feet," said one marine.

"Still goin'," said another.

The driver's body rose a hundred feet in the air, and then it stopped for a moment, and slowly started back to earth, gaining speed as it went, until the marines heard the impact as the body struck the ground.

They did not even go over to look: Another one of the friendly dead.

The marines with the 37mm gun had a new problem. One wheel of the gun was stuck. Getting it unstuck seemed the most important thing in the world just then. They fought the wheel for a while, and it came unstuck. By this time bullets were crackling around—nothing serious but they were there. The marines moved the gun to the middle of the terrace, opened the trail, and got the gun ready to fire.

A shell burst in front of the gun. The marines ignored it. A second shell came in closer, and shrapnel snarled around them. A third shell followed. The Japanese were shooting at the gun.

Sergeant Gallant jumped.

"Back off. Back off. They'll hit the gun the next time!" he shouted.

The marines scattered and threw themselves against the bank. Shells now began to fall around the gun. One blew off a wheel. An explosion on the gun knocked off the sight. The marines sat back against the bank. The gun was useless. The tractor driver had died for nothing.

So that was Sergeant Gallant's morning: a whole morning spent doing nothing at all.

CHAPTER NINE

"The Most Savage and the Most Costly Battle"

—LIEUTENANT GENERAL HOLLAND M. SMITH, USMC

Before noon, the Twenty-eighth Marines had crossed the southern end of No. 1 Airfield, and, as noted, the Twenty-seventh Marines had reached the cliffs overlooking the western beaches of the island. Mt. Suribachi was now cut off, but the marines were a long way from capturing it.

The going was much slower and much rougher for the Fourth Marine Division. The Twenty-third Marines on the left flank had gained only 500 yards by noon. Two hours later, units reached the edge of Airfield No. 1, but could not go any farther. Tanks came up but some of them suffered the same fate as Sergeant Gallant's amphtrac and were blown sky-high by powerful land mines.

On the right, the Twenty-fifth Marines attacked inland toward the airfield and north against the high ground. The old quarry above the East Boat Basin gave them a lot of trouble with many pillboxes in the cliffs. Large landing craft were brought in to spot pillboxes and bunkers for larger warships, and the big ship guns smashed many pillboxes. The craft would move in close to shore, spot a pillbox and begin firing with their machine guns, tracers guiding the gunners of the destroyers and cruisers.

The First Battalion of the Twenty-fifth Marines made only 600 yards by 11:30 on D Day. The Third Battalion, which had the northern assignment, was pinned down almost from the beginning. It was two o'clock in the afternoon before Colonel Lanigan was able to launch an attack. Later in the afternoon, the battalion reached the first ridge behind the East Boat Basin.

LSMs (landing ships medium) brought in tanks, trucks, bulldozers, and other heavy items on Beach Yellow, but one of the LSMs took at least one direct hit from enemy gunfire. Some did not even unload, but moved back out of range and waited. The fire was so heavy that on this first day the navy decided not to bring in the LSTs at all. So the supplies were transshipped into amphtracs, which could get in, and into ducks (amphibious trucks), which carried artillery in.

By eleven o'clock the Yellow beaches were piled up with wreckage so thick that the landing craft were having difficulty edging in to shore. Only the high priority items were being landed: ammunition, radio equipment and telephones, medical supplies, rations, and water. The amphtracs were carrying their supplies right up to the line—there was no time for establishing dumps—and then the taking the wounded back.

The beachmasters were on the shore with their bullhorns, trying to direct the traffic amid the roar of the rising surf and the crash of enemy shells around them. Marines and Seabees were unloading and starting to create a few dumps.

Seabees did all kinds of jobs. Some were checkers, which meant their job was to check off a list the supplies as they came in. But since some of the supplies never got there, and since the amphtracs were carrying others right up to the line, the job was foolish. So the checkers started picking up boxes of ammunition and medical supplies and taking them where they were needed.

The Seabees moved ammunition off the beach and up to the terraces. Several were killed by artillery fire, and one by a sniper.

On the beach, other Seabees trained for the job searched out and destroyed mines, blew up the wreckage, and got it away from the critical landing areas.

The Japanese artillery was fierce. Rocket trucks were unloaded into landing ships out at sea and were destroyed before they got to shore, and on the shore, artillery and other heavy equipment attracted Japanese artillery fire. A 37mm gun caught attention as it was being unloaded from the ramp of an LCVP, (landing craft, vehicles and personnel) and a shell came in and killed or wounded all the seven men handling the gun.

In the first several hours the earth-moving equipment began to come to shore and the Caterpillar tractors got to work. The Seabee operators towed bogged vehicles to shore, and some of them got going again. They dug revetments for dumps, and started to build roads along the beach and through the terraces.

When the surf began in midday, things got much worse on the beaches. Most of the supplies had to be brought in by amphibious tractors. LVTs were also used, but many of them were swamped and broached in the surf. By midafternoon, so many landing craft were wrecked and damaged that they littered the northern beaches and posed a serious hazard to traffic and supply.

On Yellow Beach One, one mortar section of the Twenty-third Marines was supplied all day long, largely through the efforts of its section leader, Gunnery Sergeant Raphael Kearns, who made trip after trip to the beach, finding amphtracs with mortar ammunition aboard and bringing them ashore for his guns.

Day waned, but the amphtracs kept working. They had to work, otherwise there would be many marines ashore without food or ammunition, because by nightfall of D Day, 30,000 men had been landed on the island.

Not only were there supplies to be brought in, but wounded to be taken out. In that first day, 519 men died or were missing and 2,420 were wounded. They had to be taken to the hospital ships. At first in the jam-up the wounded lay on the beaches, where they were subjected to Japanese mortar and artillery fire, and many of them died from wounds received after they had first been casualties.

In the afternoon virtually all the reserves were committed to the battle at the battalion and regimental levels. Even so, by the end of that first bloody battering day, the beachhead was woefully small. From the East Boat Basin it extended inland to the No. 1 Airfield and along the edges and across the southwestern end to the west beaches, and returning to the east beaches along the northern foothills of Mt. Suribachi. The beachhead was only 4,000 yards long and 700 yards deep in the north, and 1,100 yards deep in the south, and it housed six infantry regiments, six artillery battalions, and two tank battalions.

The Fourth Division landing zones stretched from halfway up the north shore to the high cliffs above the East Boat Basin. The whole defense here was one mass of concrete pillboxes and bunkers, with coastal defense guns and artillery and mortars and automatic weapons in the maze of caverns and caves.

The First Battalion of the Twenty-third Infantry ran into many land mines. The Second Battalion did, too. The First Battalion of the Twenty-fifth Marines pushed toward the quarry to gain six hundred yards off the beach and up the slopes. The Second Battalion of the Twenty-fourth Marines advanced through rocks and caves, taking heavy casualties. By nightfall, most of the company commanders and platoon leaders were dead or wounded, and most of the noncoms were also gone. Company I lost six officers. By 4:40 in the afternoon, all the officers of K Company were cut down. When the Second Battalion crossed the beach, it was nearly one thousand men strong. By nightfall only three hundred were still in action.

The highest ranking officer to come ashore on D Day was Brigadier General Leo Hermle, assistant commander of the Fifth Marine Division. Like so many others, his small boat milled around because the beaches were full, and it was three o'clock that afternoon before he was able to establish a command post near the south end of Airfield No. 1. What he saw when he came in was enough to convince him that the fight for Iwo Jima was going to be very long and arduous. When he got set up, he radioed General Rockey aboard the ship *Athene* to stay where he was at least until morning. There was nothing he could do on Iwo Jima right now, except possibly get killed.

After that decision, General Hermle sent runners out to the battalions to tell them to consolidate and set up perimeters for the night, and to expect serious counterattacks from the enemy after dark.

The Most Savage and the Most Costly Battle 69

General Kuribayashi followed the battle from his headquarters blockhouse at the northern end of Iwo Jima. So far, the battle had gone as he wanted it to. The enemy had been met on the beaches, and although he knew from studying all the other island battles that they would not be stopped there, they had been sorely hurt. Night fell, but the Japanese artillery never went to sleep. All night long they would send shells all over the marine positions.

The general informed Tokyo that night that he was "slaughtering" the invaders.

CHAPTER TEN

Night

Darkness settled over the island and, based on their previous experience, the marines waited for counterattack, which in the past had often taken the form of infiltration during the early evening hours, followed by a series of *banzai* charges.

Aboard the command ship *Eldorado*, Lieutenant General Holland M. Smith was expecting a Japanese counterattack this first night.

"We will welcome a counterattack. That is generally when we break their backs," he said.

Down by Mt. Suribachi, the Twenty-eighth Marines prepared to spend a dangerous and cold and cheerless night. Virtually all of them had discarded their packs and blanket rolls on the perilous passage across the island, and now they found themselves shivering in their cotton fatigue uniforms, and without food. The shore parties were working that night to bring supplies. A group of amphibious army trucks, manned by black soldiers, came onto the beach north of Suribachi and encountered a marine supply sergeant. He suggested that they take their supplies inland and they agreed, so they made a sweep behind the front lines, dropping water, ammunition, and rations, as they went.

None of this supply came to E Company of the Second Battalion of the Twenty-eighth Marines. The men of Lieutenant Wells's platoon had chosen a Japanese trench for their first night's lodging on the island. Actually it was two trenches and Corporal Wheeler's squad occupied the intersection. The men huddled in three arms of the trenches, on the left flank of the platoon. The fourth arm of the trench led off toward the Japanese bunker area and this was guarded by the squad BAR (Browning Automatic Rifle) man, Private First Class Edward Kurelik. The squad leader assigned watches, so that at least one man would be awake and alert at all times. Then the marines settled down to try to get some rest, fearful of the night and what it might bring.

The warmth of day evaporated in the night air and it turned cold. Actually the temperature was about 60 degrees Fahrenheit, but the marines had been training in Hawaii and other tropical climates and 60 degrees was cold. They thought about the packs they had discarded on the way across the island, with the blankets and field jackets. The packs also contained their rations, but none of them cared about that. They were too keyed up to want to eat.

Shortly after dark, they heard voices, and a group of men appeared on the edge of the perimeter. Obviously American, they were talking in loud tones and making sure that they were heard, so no bullets would begin coming their way. They were marines, obviously engaged on some special mission. They passed along the perimeter and out of earshot, and the talking suddenly ceased. They did not reappear.

From the ships, star shells began to go up, and occasionally firing from a ship or from the artillery on the beach punctuated the night. From time to time, the Japanese fired, but seemed to be shooting at nothing in particular, just shooting at the beachhead. And sometimes from guns on Mt. Suribachi some shells would come in, but never close enough to worry the men of the platoon.

The flashes and the naval shells gave the men glimpses of Mt. Suribachi, which was their assigned objective. The volcano stood about a third of a mile from where Easy Company was dug in. It seemed a long long way. The afternoon attack had been a failure. The open terrain, the slippery sand, the blockhouses and pillboxes, and the stubborn Japanese defense had combined to prevent them from making progress. The attack had been scheduled for 3:45, but had not even begun until nearly five o'clock, and it seemed that as soon as it had been launched the word had been passed to call it off.

Wheeler's squad had it lucky. Not all the company had such comfortable or relatively safe quarters. They could see two other marines, a BAR man and a corporal, who had been ordered to occupy a barren knob that stuck up above the bushes. It was a high point and necessary to guard, but it was also very tough going. These two were completely exposed. They tried to dig in, but the knob was hard rock and unyielding to their entrenching tools. They could not even scrabble down to get a shallow hole, but lay up there on the top, exposed.

The night dragged on. From time to time, volleys of rifle fire could be herd on the mountain. What were the Japanese shooting at? Some of the time they seemed to be shooting at the battalion, but they never came near Wells's platoon. The men could also hear the sounds of firing elsewhere on the island, and the firing of the marine artillery. But it all seemed unreal and nothing to worry much about. Their concentration was on sounds, listening for the scratching and scraping noises that would indicate Japanese on the move. For everyone expected at least one night attack from the Japanese infantry. The intelligence briefings had indicated that the enemy had a large force of infantry on the island and many tanks. And this was the night to hit the marines, who did not know the terrain, while the defenders knew every inch of it. The marines were only shakily established on the island.

After midnight, to the north, there was a sudden burst of heavy artillery fire from the marine guns, and Wheeler's squad knew that something was going on. Later they learned that the Japanese defenders in that area had defied their general and had started to stage a *banzai* attack against the Twenty-seventh Marines, just north of the Twenty-eighth's position. The Japanese were organizing along a 500-yard front when they were discovered, and the marine artillery laid down a barrage that killed a large number of enemy troops and put a stop to the night action before it got started.

Night 73

An hour or so later, more excitement came. This was much closer, and it involved the First Battalion of the Twenty-eight Marines, bedded down between Wells's platoon and Mt. Suribachi. First came Japanese sounds, and then a hail of rifle and machine gun and mortar fire. The First Battalion had discovered a Japanese barge loaded with troops trying to make a landing on the west coast, between Easy Company and the mountain. The barge was attacked and about twenty-five Japanese soldiers were killed, which put an end to that effort.

Still Easy Company waited for the big night attack.

Farther inland, other elements of the company were camped among the neutralized pillboxes. One BAR man saw three Japanese moving up to one pillbox. One man was standing at the base, and the other two were creeping up toward the opening at the top. The BAR man fired at the man standing at the bottom and killed him. He swung the BAR up the slope and began firing, but was blinded by his muzzle blast. He killed one of the Japanese, but the third man escaped.

In the trench, Corporal Wheeler lay shivering, with his rifle in his hands and his combat knife stuck in the sand of the trench. His segment of the trench was not quite whole. Part of the trench had been blown away by the explosion of a shell, and he faced a slope, not a solid wall. He lay waiting, watching, expecting at any moment to see a Japanese face come up on the far side of the slope. But when the Japanese finally did come, it was not that way.

Not far away occurred an incident of the sort that Lieutenant Wells had warned about. One marine was crouched in a shell hole, when a Japanese infiltrator slipped in beside him. He jumped up, shouted "Jap! Jap!" and ran for another hole. Another marine saw him running and shot him, believing he was the Japanese infiltrator. The Japanese escaped in the excitement.

BAR man Kurelik was covering his trench as ordered. Suddenly Corporal Wheeler was alerted by Kurelik's voice.

"Studebaker!" he shouted.

Corporal Wheeler knew that something was up. This was the challenge agreed upon.

Where was the answer?

The answer came in an exclamation in Japanese, followed by the flash and sound of an exploding grenade. Kurelik was hit by shrapnel, and so was one other marine of the squad. The others jumped up and began firing into the shadows, and Sergeant Snyder, the squad leader, threw two grenades. But there was no response, and no further sound from the trench.

Corporal Wheeler sat down again in the trench and discovered that his teeth were chattering. He clamped them tight, and held them until the spasm went away. By that time, one of the platoon corpsman was working his way along the trench on hands and knees, shouting as he came so that the marines would not shoot him. He got to the two wounded men, and found that Kurelik had a hole in his thigh and a fractured foot. The other marine had only superficial skin wounds.

Sergeant Snyder decided the chances of more trouble were very high, and so he placed a second BAR man at the danger point in the trench, and told him not to worry about the recognition signal. If he heard something moving in that trench he was to open fire. So the men of the squad settled down to watch and wait. But nothing else happened and eventually morning came.

In other sectors there were little bits of excitement. The Japanese had organized "wolf packs" of three or four men, who were detailed to harry the Americans this night. They slipped through the lines, with the mission of blowing up American supply dumps. One team reached a Fourth Division dump that contained ammunition, gasoline and flamethrower fluid. They blew a grenade, and the whole dump exploded with an enormous roar and flash that could be seen all over the island. Foxholes in the area were collapsed, and several marines nearly suffocated.

Down on the beach, a Seabee was looking at the surf when a log came floating down from the north, borne by the current. It seemed harmless until it suddenly made a sharp turn. The Seabee opened fire with his rifle, and a dead Japanese tumbled off the log.

In another part of the beach, a sunken Japanese vessel had been looked over several times that day, and nothing had been found. But that night, the artillery and mortar fire in the north and central part of the island was directed by a Japanese radio operator working from the sunken craft. He had been hiding there all day, and this night he came out to direct the artillery fire. Marines on the beach heard the clicking of the radio, and they crept up on the vessel, attacked and shot the operator.

Up north, a Japanese naval officer ordered a squad of sailors to make a reconnaissance of the beaches to the south, and they set out, avoiding the marines as well as they could, checking the beaches to see what had happened there. They passed the wreckage of the amphtracs and the landing boats, and marveled at the earth-moving equipment on the shore. They reached a spot on one terrace that overlooked the southernmost beach, and this was as far as they had been told to come. They saw the Seabees and the sailors still unloading on the southern beach in the night. They passed a Seabee sentry, armed with a BAR, but he did not see them. The Japanese slipped back into their own lines, to be hit by an American shell. One man was badly hurt and his companions carried him to an aid station, and then reported on what they had seen to their officer.

The marines in the northern part of the island had it worst from enemy shelling. A direct hit fell on the command post of the First Battalion of the Twenty-third Marines, killing the battalion commander and his operations officer.

Second Lieutenant Cyril Zurlinden, a public relations officer, was lying in a shell hole about 200 yards from the front when a shell hit very close, breaking his leg and twisting it. When he saw the leg he thought it belonged to another body and tried to throw it out of his hole. He then learned. It was morning before a corpsman reached him, and he was taken back to a ship for surgery. Surprisingly, he did not lose the leg.

Except for the infiltrators and some enthusiastic Japanese who had tried the failed attacks, General Kuribayashi's men spent a quiet night in their caves deep underground, eating their evening meal and drinking *sake*. The general was pleased with the way the first day's battle had gone. He knew from looking at the beach that he was inflicting serious damage on his enemies. He sent another message to Tokyo that night, full of confidence. "We are annihilating the enemy," he said.

CHAPTER ELEVEN

The Second Phase

Surveying the results of the first day's battle at Iwo Jima, Lieutenant General Holland M. Smith was not happy. Before the invasion, he had observed that this was going to be a very tough nut to crack, and had asked for all the extra bombardment he could get. The navy had delivered all that it could for three days, but still it was not enough and "Howling Mad" Smith complained. But the fact was that the fault did not lie with navy failure, but with the nature of General Kuribayashi's powerful defenses. As the gunners of the big ships had learned ruefully, nothing less than a direct hit would knock out the blockhouses and the guns in their thick revetments. The Japanese general had a lot more respect for the bombardment.

"I am not afraid of the fighting power of only three American marine divisions," said Kuribayashi, "if there is no bombardment from aircraft and warships. That is the only reason why we have to face such miserable situations."

That night of February 19, the marine division and regimental commanders pored over their maps and selected the targets they wanted hit by the bombardment the next morning. Each marine battalion had at least one destroyer assigned, with a marine liaison officer aboard, and a navy shore fire control party with the marine unit. At daybreak, the navy came in again and the big ships began to work over the shore installations they knew about. Four battleships, three cruisers and an LCI mortar team hit their targets from 7:40 in the morning until

8:30. Then the marines set about their day's task. Spotting planes circled apparently lazily in the sky, looking for other targets. The difficult targets were hard to spot. Usually they remained exposed just as their guns were firing, and then they buttoned up again.

That morning Colonel Lanigan's men of the Twenty-fifth Marines and Colonel Wensinger's Twenty-third were ordered to move out at 8:30.

The battle was developing into two distinct operations. In the south, three battalions of the Twenty-eighth Marines occupied a line across the neck of the island, facing south towards Mt. Suribachi. Just to the north of them, the Twenty-sixth and Twenty-seventh Marines were across the southern tip of Airport No. 1. On the right of these regiments were the three regiments of the Fourth Marine Division.

The Third Marine Division was still at sea, in floating reserve. That morning the artillery naval gunfire and air attack preparations for the assault on Mt. Suribachi began soon after daybreak. The drive north would come at the same time. The front lines were now marked with panels of white cloth to direct the airmen.

The attacks north and south on the mountain were begun together at 8:30, the riflemen moving forward with fixed bayonets, covered where possible by mortar and machine gun fire, and demolition men with charges and flamethrowers.

The confusion of D Day had left its mark. The tanks were not able to operate this day yet because their maintenance sections were not on shore. Company C of the Fifth Tank Battalion attached to the Twenty-eighth Infantry had eight tanks, but no fuel or ammunition for them. They salvaged some of both from knocked out tanks, and tried to get going. But the Japanese put down a heavy mortar barrage on the tanks, and when they moved the barrage moved with them. This happened three times. There was no place the marines could move to where they could not be seen by the Japanese observers on Mt. Suribachi.

This was also true of the infantry. The left half of the line had to cross open sand, and the right side went through scrub. The heaviest defenses were at the base of the mountain, but the cave and tunnel entrances all the way up hid some artillery pieces, mortars, and machine guns.

There was only one way to go up the mountain. It had to be a frontal assault against an enemy that was hidden and powerful.

That afternoon of D Day + 1, Captain Roscoe Good estimated the numbers of the defense to be almost as great as those of the offense.

Lieutenant Colonel Chandler Johnson's Second Battalion of the Twenty-eighth Marines attacked that morning on the left and the Third Battalion on the right. The Second Battalion, which had done the heaviest fighting the day before, was held in reserve.

Johnson had a habit of rushing back and forth looking for trouble spots, and it may have saved his life this morning. He was up front when his command post in the rear was hit by mortar fire which killed several men.

The tanks got into the fight at eleven o'clock that morning, and behind them were the 37mm guns and 75mm half-tracks of the regimental weapons company. In the rear were the artillerymen of Forty-third Battalion of the Thirteenth Marines. Ships on both sides of the mountain threw shells into Suribachi, and the aircraft of the carriers attacked the mountain. But the Japanese positions were very well guarded, and their artillery was still strong. By noon, the attack had only gained seventy-five yards. In the afternoon they gained another 125 yards. The First Battalion of the Twenty-eighth came along to mop up and killed about seventy-five Japanese who had been harassing the troops up ahead of them. No innocent-looking sand mounds were left undisturbed, and they often contained live Japanese soldiers. The Japanese could be anywhere. In the middle of the afternoon, Sergeant Hap Mowrey took a patrol to meet a half-track that was coming from the beach loaded with ammunition and food. They were taking fire from Mt. Suribachi at the time, and they skirted their way until the found the half-track and started back up front. As they got close to their company, they saw Japanese soldiers, and one of the patrol jumped to the half-track machine gun and sprayed the area. Then Mowrey saw a Japanese arm lift, and a grenade. The grenade knocked him off his feet; his rifle and helmet spun away. He had been hit in the chest and abdomen. They got him to an aid station and he survived.

Lieutenant Bates was still in action, even with his broken arm, knocking out gun emplacements with the help of some engineers. The engineers looked for land mines, and three were blown up by them. The marines came up to the big gun installation, which was protected by machine gun nests, and one by one destroyed the machine guns. They then threw satchel charges into the ventilator of the bunker. The Japanese began flinging hand grenades, and some wounded soldiers came around the edge of the bunker. The marines tried to fire, but their weapons were jammed with sand scattered by the grenades. The Japanese turned and ran into a machine gun the marines had set up. The marines moved around the bunker and found more Japanese, who tried to pull the pins on grenades. Most of the marines' rifles were jammed with sand so they could not shoot the Japanese, but one man got his piece going and then he shot them all. The marines blew up the barrel of the big gun with a charge.

The 216th and Twenty-seventh Marines were moving north toward the center of the airfield and across it. They began that morning with their left flank on the western shore of the island and their right flank about 1000 yards inland. Here the open terrain did not lend itself to heavy fortification, but there were bunkers and pillboxes strung about, and the area was full of land mines. The Japanese had the land sited for artillery and mortar barrages, and these came in frequently. Still, the marines of the two regiments moved forward 800 yards that day.

But every yard was a struggle. One tank had a track torn off by a land mine. When the commander opened the turret to see what had happened, he saw a Japanese soldier in the brush, raising his rifle. He shot the Japanese with his 45 caliber. He and the crew then jumped out. Several other Japanese soldiers were right there, and the Americans managed to kill all of them.

Attacking to the right of the Twenty-sixth and Twenty-seventh Marines, the left wing of the Fourth Division moved up the center of the island sweeping toward the north end of the No. 1 Airport. The Japanese would disappear on the south edge of the airport. They were going into tunnels which ran through the airport, and they came out the other side to fight again. Some of the Japanese moved slowly back across the airfield, taking shelter in wrecked planes and sniping from them until wiped out individually.

The No. 1 Airport was captured by noon, and then the attack moved toward the southern tip of the No. 2 Airport and the southern end of the Japanese main line of defense.

The captain of the battleship *Washington* had a report of a strong point of enemy resistance near the southern end of Airfield No. 2. An air-spotting plane was sent to take a look, and the observer reported back that there were a lot of pillboxes over there. That was the understatement of the day. The Japanese defenders had built more than three hundred pillboxes, bunkers, and infantry shelters in a space five hundred yards wide and a thousand yards long. Besides these, they had dug caves into the cliff, facing what was now the marine front line. They were looking right down the throats of the Twenty-fifth Marines.

This was the sort of situation in which the big guns of the battleship could do some real good. The air-spotter directed the gunners to start with the main battery of 16-inch guns at one end of the cliff. Then he called for salvoes at fifty-yard intervals. The 16-inch shells penetrated the mountain and ate away the cliff. The loose gravel began to roll, and it sealed up many of the cave mouths, with the Japanese inside.

This system was so successful that the *Washington* stayed on the firing line for ten hours that day, firing both its 16-inch and secondary batteries. Knocking out the man-made pillboxes was tougher, because they had been carefully built of reinforced concrete with sand to cover and take up the impact of artillery shells. It took a direct hit, preferably in the aperture, to do the job. Hits on top too often glanced off harmlessly from the sand. The satchel charge, the thermite grenade, the 75mm gun of the tanks, and the flamethrower were more effective.

The men of the Twenty-fifth Marines did not know it when they came off Beach Blue, but they were heading right into the Japanese main line of defense. Progress was a question of moving up to a pillbox, digging in, firing, and sending somebody forward to blow the pillbox, trying at the same time to knock it out with a mortar or a gun. With three hundred such installations in this little area, it took a lot of time, and cost a lot of blood.

On the afternoon of D Day, the weather had taken a turn for the worse for the invaders, and the surf had come up to scatter the landing craft and make it hard for the coxswains to hold them on a lee shore. The day dawned quiet on D Day + 1, but by noon, it had begun to rough up and the weather had changed again, to become ever more disadvantageous. The wind moved around from southeast to southwest and built up to twenty miles an hour. Then a cold front came by and the wind changed to northeast, raising a heavy sea. On the beach the wrecked landing craft began to float around, smashing into incoming boats. The only way to get any vehicular traction on the beaches was to put down metal marston matting, but there was not enough of this to go along the beach, and it always seemed that where it was wanted most was just where it was not available. Salvage parties were among the busiest men on the beach, pulling wrecked vehicles out of the way, getting rid of wrecked landing craft, and trying to deal with incoming congestion, all of this while under fire from mortars and enemy shelling.

The driving force on the beach was Captain Carl E. Anderson, known as "Squeaky" from his high-pitched voice. He was an old salvage man from civil life, as profane as he was high-voiced, and he marched up and down the beach in his own particular uniform, shouting and gesticulating, moving bulldozers and tanks around to get wreckage out of the way. The uniform would have gotten him cashiered in the peacetime navy: cut-off pants held up by a gun belt, black navy-issue socks and shoes, and garters. But nobody complained, and if there had been complaint, it would have been silenced by the grateful marines.

On the left and across on the west side of Iwo Jima the men of the Second Battalion of Colonel Liversedge's Twenty-eighth

The Second Phase 83

Marines had only one thought on their minds—to get up Mt. Suribachi and get the Japanese out of there. On D Day, Lieutenant Colonel Chandler Johnson had taken them off the beach in short order. With him was Second Lieutenant Greeley Wells, who was carrying an American flag borrowed from one of the transports. They intended to plant that flag at the top of the volcano.

But it wasn't going to happen in a big hurry. That morning, the destroyer *Mannert L. Abele* and minelayer *Thomas E. Fraser* started putting in neutralizing fire at 7:15, and kept it up for four hours and fifteen minutes, from a point 1,500 yards off the beach. That morning they fired 1,700 rounds of 5-inch ammunition at the base of the mountain, in support of the assault of the Twenty-eighth Marines. In spite of that, the marines gained only fifty yards that morning against the pillboxes and caves. But those fortifications were so close to the front line that much of the routing of the Japanese had to be done by the infantry, and by the tanks when they came at about 11 A.M. Still, altogether the Twenty-eighth Marines gained only about 200 yards that second day of the assault. At the end of the day, the marines held a line that went across the island above Mt. Suribachi and included the No. 1 Airfield. But to the north they were stopped on the slopes of the bulge, by the main line of defense. All six regiments of the Fourth and Fifth Marine Divisions were ashore.

During the night of February 20, destroyers and cruisers again came in to light up the area and carry out harassing fire on the known Japanese areas, while again the rest of the warships withdrew to deep water, to return at dawn.

On February 21, the morning began with rain and a twenty-mile-an-hour wind that brought heavy surf on the beach. The morning bombardment began at 7:40 and continued for half an hour.

Japanese artillery fire had slowed down considerably, so the larger supply vessels capable of reaching the beach, the LSMs and LSTs, were able to come in to the beach for the first time and unload supplies directly instead of decanting them into amphtracs. That day, the building of supply dumps began, and the artillery no longer had to suspend firing while somebody scouted up some more ammunition. Day and night the beachmasters and their gangs worked to build supply dumps, clear the wreckage, and bring in landing craft. The bulldozers were ashore, and they were building roads along the beach. As the marine line moved farther from the landing beaches, the problems of getting supplies to the front troops became more complicated, and the shore party commanders had the job of keeping things moving, and of bringing the casualties down to the beach in a hurry for evacuation to the ships. Two thousand Seabees were ashore by this time. Public address systems set up on the beach sent out interesting conversations that must have been confusing to the Japanese: directing traffic, calling for corpsmen to bring casualties to the beach, sorting out the loaded and unloaded landing craft, and warning off craft when the beaches got too full. There was no shelter for the supply dumps, and the Japanese gunners tried to search them out with their artillery. When they hit a gasoline or ammunition dump the results were spectacular, with parts of vehicles and smoke rising hundreds of feet in the air. The beach was shelled almost constantly, and every once in a while an enemy barrage would connect with something important. Nobody in the beach parties complained, because the talkers kept reminding them that the marines on the line were getting it ten times as heavy.

At dawn on D + 2, the Twenty-fourth Marines were ashore with the other two regiments of the Fourth Battalion, so the ready reserves were committed and the division was prepared to make a new effort to forge ahead against General Kuribayashi's still largely hidden defense line.

"Stand by to move out. Pass the word."

It went down the line. The marines had been routed out by the sergeants. They had picked up their ponchos and started to fold them. Now they went back to their shelters and began to assemble their gear. They looked over their rifles, rolled up their ponchos, adjusted their gas mask carriers on their backs, and put on their caps, helmets, and liners. For most of them, this routine was old by now, but it was new to be doing it here on an island in the middle of the Pacific and knowing that this was real, and not a drill. This time it counted. This time the helmet meant something. They were going into battle. They picked up their grenades and hung them on their belts and pockets, and made sure they had their cartridge belts. Some men had extra cartridge belts, just in case.

The marines sat around the edges of their night shelters and waited. The Japanese mortars and the artillery were beginning to boom again this morning, but they were a long way off. That was good. The marine artillery was firing over their heads and the shells were falling where the Japanese were supposed to be. That was better.

The old hands offered little bits of advice.

"Ours are pack howitzers. Ya gotta learn how they sound. Hear?"

Another noise, very much the same.

"That was one of theirs. Hear the difference? No? Well, LISTEN! Goddam it! Ya gotta learn to hear. It don't make no difference right now. Long ways away. But it will. It will."

Gradually the new ones learned to recognize the pack howitzers, firing four at time, one after the other: first a sizzling noise, then a *thunk*, as the projectile came out of the barrel, then a space of time, and then a wham as the projectile exploded somewhere out in front. Just now the sizzling was almost constant, because all the howitzers were firing, battery by battery.

"Wait'll they bring the one-oh-fives ashore, then you'll hear something. They'll knock the hell out of the Jap artillery."

Actually, they had tried to bring the 155s ashore that day for the Fourth Division, but in the high seas, the guns of the Third and Fourth Battalions of the Fourteenth Marines did not fare well. Of the twelve guns, only two got ashore. The Fifth Division was luckier; they got four 155mm howitzers delivered on the wreckage of Beach Red and worked across the terraces toward the west coast.

Perhaps on D + 2 with these they could blast the Japanese. This day, D + 1, for big guns the troops were still dependent on the ships, which were doing a good job. One emplacement high on the hillside in the northern area of the cross island defenses held ten 20mm antiaircraft guns that gave the incoming carrier

86 IWO JIMA

planes a bad time and hit a number of them. Spotters located this gun emplacement, and around four o'clock on the afternoon of D + 1, the battleship *Washington* took the guns under fire with its 16-inch battery. The Japanese had retreated to their shelter far underground for the afternoon. When they came up in the evening, all ten of their guns had been destroyed.

Elsewhere, although the 16-inch and the 8-inch and the 5-inch guns of the fleet were firing, the Japanese were still firing, too. This world was a cacaphony of gunfire with the battleship guns, like kettledrums and cymbals all rolled into one, going *crack-boom, crack-boom* overhead, so near and so loud that the new men flinched every time a 16-inch gun spoke up.

Every once in a while an LCT would come in and let loose a flock of rockets, and the noise was like a dozen Fourth of Julys. *Whoosh whoosh whoosh whoosh wham wham wham wham.* Sometimes there were a hundred rockets in the air, and when they hit, one after the other, the hillside and the mountain erupted in clouds of smoke and dust. The planes of the carriers were overhead, hitting up there just ahead of the line, much nearer, sending off their rockets, and following up with the crackle of machine gun fire, and the zoom as they dived and pulled out.

The marines waited for their orders.

Then came the word to one platoon:

"Stand by for tank attack."

The men were alarmed.

They weren't ready for tanks. What were they going to do?

The question was answered when the platoon sergeant spoke.

"All right men. This is what we're gonna do." He squatted down and the men moved in a circle around him.

"The platoon is gonna pull back here." He pointed to the terrace about thirty yards in back of them. "Spotters will go along the ridge, and the rest of us will pull back here."

The sergeant looked around.

He called names.

"You two guys get up here on the right and watch. Watch everything ahead and to the right. Somebody else will be on your left. Keep your eyes open, for Chrissakes. If you see

The Second Phase 87

anything, then pass the word and run like hell. Understand?"

The two who had been singled out nodded mutely.

The sergeant nodded. "Get up there and keep your eyes open."

One of the spotters moved up the bank straight ahead, scooped a shallow hollow out of the gravel on the right side of the incline, and sat down with his back to it, watching the ground ahead. It was level for about hundred yards, and then it dissolved into a series of little hills covered with scrub.

The other spotter climbed the bank and moved into familiar territory, a foxhole which had been occupied by three marines of the squad the night before. The two right hand spotters were about five yards apart. On their left were two other spotters from the platoon. They were standing on the ridge line, and the top halves of their bodies stuck up over the ridge.

A corporal came up and talked to one of the spotters. Then he went over to the left hand spotters. The second spotter went to join the first, to find out what was going on. And it was too lonesome where he was, all by himself. Nobody had said they had to be in separate holes, they just said to watch.

It started to rain. The spotters put their heads down, but then they couldn't see. So they put their heads up, and the water trickled down their faces and their noses. The water from the rain turned the lava sand into lava mud, and it stuck to their hands and got on their faces. Where their hands touched their weapons they made muddy streaks.

It got cold. The water dripped down onto their legs and wet their clothes, and the combat fatigues got cold and wet and made them shiver. Both of them were trembling from cold and fear. The cold started it, and the fear intensified it.

They made a few jokes and they relaxed. They decided they were shivering from the cold, not from fear. At least, that's what they told each other.

They stopped talking because the American barrage began. The sizzling and *thunks* and *whams* of their own artillery barrage were joined by the bigger guns of the ships. The hills ahead of them erupted in columns of smoke, and a haze developed over the ground ahead. The American mortars joined in, and the barrage moved up to the hills and then back again toward them, stopped and moved up again.

One column of smoke rose high behind the hills. They said to each other that somebody got a tank. Maybe. But they saw no tanks and they saw no Japanese.

Then the barrage began again, and some of the shells began to strike within fifty yards of the hole they were in. They burrowed down in the shell hole and put their faces against the dirt, looking up to do their job only when the barrage died away. They looked around. The other spotters on their left were gone. One of the spotters went on back to the platoon while the other waited. The first spotter came back and gestured, and the second spotter followed him back to the platoon.

One of the other two spotters had been hit in the face, and he lay on the ground with half a dozen men around him. He bled from the face and neck. A corpsman was tending to him, and had already sent down to the beach for a stretcher.

The squad huddled in little groups around the crest of the bank. The rain had stopped during the barrage. Now they had dug in here in shallow holes in the slope. Off to the left, the terrace turned, and below them, under its protection, stood a tank that had been put out of action up front and brought back here for repair. Members of the crew in their helmets and tanker's boots stood around the tank and waited. The rest of the platoon was strung out behind on the slope.

The sizzling began again, but this time it was Japanese fire, which seemed to be searching for the American artillery. Some of the men continued to dig, but most of them just lay in the shallow foxholes waiting.

The artillery fire probed but remained far from their position. It was the mortars that came close, and several shells fell around the tank in back of them, so that the sergeant finally came up and told everybody to get away from the tank because the Japs were aiming at it.

In intervals, the men moved around and exchanged scuttlebutt. They learned that one of their lieutenants had been killed and the captain had been wounded. So had the company first sergeant.

The Second Phase 89

The platoon moved up that afternoon, into a minefield. It had been vetted by the demolitions men who had marked the mines with little strings of cloth tied to sticks. But in the afternoon shadows it was hard to see the bits of cloth, so everybody walked very cautiously, passing the word whenever they saw anything unusual.

They moved up, running through the open spaces and throwing themselves down in the first cover they could see. One of the marines landed almost on top of a dead Japanese in a shell hole. He had been eviscerated and his hands were gone.

Their company was moving to the right, someone said, and they were going into the line at the right. They wished they would get there, because it was growing darker all the time, and it was hard to see where they were going. They moved by column now, and turned to the left, moving up the ascending slope from the beach in a long snaky line. A Japanese machine gun began to fire, and the marines in front hurled themselves into a communications trench. The gun kept firing, and the men kept piling up in the trench. The first comers yelled at them to stay back but on they came, so the first men ducked out and ahead, afraid that the Japanese would begin loading mortar fire into the trench. They sought shell holes ahead for safety.

The sound of mortars and machine gun fire was punctuated now with the crack of the 25 caliber Japanese rifles and the crump of grenades. These men were in the front line, and had gotten there without knowing it.

The squad watched as a sergeant and a corporal from the second squad were up against a pillbox, and were engaging it. A Japanese rifle grenade suddenly exploded on the edge of their shell hole and threw fragments all around. They heard the heavy explosion of a satchel charge and saw a smoke cloud go up ahead, with fragments of something heavy going up, too.

Several marines appeared near the pillbox, and one threw a grenade inside. It exploded and dust flew up. Another did the same. The marines then raced back to safety.

Another Japanese pillbox stood at the crest of the hill. A Japanese soldier suddenly appeared at the rear of the pillbox and his arm arched. He was throwing a grenade.

"Grenade," came the shout. "Grenade."

"Shoot the sonofabitch."

"Get down."

Several marines stood up and raised their rifles. The Japanese appeared again, but was gone again before they could fire.

The second grenade hit the ground and everybody dropped. The grenade went off, but since it was on the ground the force went outward and upward. Against the ground the men were not likely to get hit.

A marine in the line twisted the ring of a grenade and threw it overhand like a baseball catcher snapping a throw to second. The grenade disappeared over the pillbox, but a Jap threw it back, and it came down in the open. The squad ducked. It exploded almost immediately.

The marines surrounded the pillbox. Obviously it was full of Japanese soldiers. They moved cautiously up. Another grenade exploded and the cry came "Corpsman. Corpsman!"

Somebody was wounded.

The pillbox on the ridge was protected by two others, one on each side of it, so the men could not go around it. They had to have more men to hit the pillbox all at once. The sergeant realized this and pulled the marines back.

The darkness was coming fast, so they dug in back there in the safe zone, and settled down for another night on Iwo Jima.

CHAPTER TWELVE

The Most Dangerous Game

The night of D + 1 was a copy of the first night. The marines expected *banzai* attacks, and none came. Their commanders counted the casualties, and were again appalled. The Americans now had control of about a fourth of the island, not the most important fourth, and they had another thousand killed and wounded to show for it. They had no conception of the Japanese casualties. They could count only about 650 Japanese dead. They knew there must be more than that, but General Kuribayashi's campaign of silence was effective. Not knowing brought a little more tension, a little more worry.

That night the Japanese artillery fired on the beaches and on the marines ashore. A big ammunition dump on the shore went up with an enormous explosion and then subsidiary explosions that sent fireworks across the beach for an hour.

Infiltration attacks were made in the Suribachi area. Defenders were seen massing on a plateau on the eastern base, and the destroyer *Henry A. Wiley* came in to a point 200 yards off the beach, switched on a searchlight, and began firing all its guns that would bear. The Japanese were completely surprised, and the incipient attack was broken up.

Here and there individual Japanese appeared to try to attack, and marines engaged them in hand-to-hand combat.

Work continued all night on the beaches, but very little cargo came in. It was as if the invasion had reached

92 IWO JIMA

a point of temporary exhaustion and had to be sparked up again.

On the morning of D + 2 Admiral Turner and General Smith were sending in the Twenty-first Marines of the Third Marine Division, the floating reserve for this invasion. They had hoped during the first part of D + 1 that they would be able to get along without it, and save it fresh for the coming operation on Okinawa. But by afternoon it was apparent that it was needed on Iwo Jima, and an attempt had been made to land the men. But the seas were so high in the loading area that some of the men fell into the water climbing down into the landing craft and had to be fished out, and when the wind came up and the conditions on the beach did not improve substantially the landing was cancelled for the day. Today they came in to the center of the line, between the Fifth Division in the south and the Fourth Division in the north.

If the marine riflemen of the Twenty-fourth Regiment thought they were having it tough as they went into the line, they should have seen what their friends of the regimental Scout-Sniper Platoon were doing.

This was the "tough jobs" unit. When the command wanted to find out what they were up against, or when they needed to know what was around that corner, the men of the Scout-Sniper Platoon were called.

On D + 2 the platoon went in to Iwo, but there wasn't anything in particular for them to do for the first few hours while the Twenty-fourth got organized on the beach and found out what was going on. So they made themselves useful. Two of them were sent to one of the new dumps to get some rations. They found a Japanese there and shot him. They poked around in caves and found some Japanese ammunition and weapons and Molotov cocktails. They left some grenades in the cave and blew them as they went out. And they whiled away D + 2.

For the marines in the center and north, D + 2 was a day of frustration. The Japanese defenses were very powerful, and virtually no gains were made.

A typical action came in the Twenty-fourth area, which was held up by six pillboxes. Two tanks came up, but both hit mines and were stopped. A gunner and six of his men came up dragging a 37mm gun, but later, after an attack by mortar and machine gun from the pillboxes, three men were out of action and one was dead. The other four men managed to get the gun firing and knocked out the pillboxes, one by one. It was a long process before the infantry could move at all.

Two Medals of Honor and many Navy Crosses were won that day in the Fifth Division. Purple Hearts were common, with so many wounded that the movement forward was excruciatingly slow. But down in the south, the attack on Mt. Suribachi began in earnest this third day of the battle. The marines were only about 200 yards from the main defense line of Mt. Suribachi, so close that the rock and debris from the naval shelling fell back near the marines in their foxholes. The attack would be made that morning by the whole regiment, the Second Battalion on the left, Third Battalion in the center and First Battalion on the right.

The bombardment ended with a strike by forty carrier planes against the base of the mountain. They came in with rockets and created so much smoke and noise that the marines were temporarily blinded and deafened. The volcano was hidden by a cloud of smoke.

When the planes had disappeared, the marines looked around for the tank support that was supposed to have come up. But the tanks had not yet arrived, and it was 8:25, time for the jumpoff. Along a 700-yard front the marines began to move under cover of firing from the artillery behind them.

The Japanese on Mt. Suribachi began to move, too, and the crackle of rifles and chattering of machine guns filled the air again. The mortars then began to add their heavier sound to the action, and mortar rounds could be seen moving in the air.

The easiest going was on the right, where the First Battalion moved ahead, but in the center and on the left the resistance was stiff. Company E of the Second Battalion was on the right side of the battalion. The Third Platoon moved out first, and the Second Platoon moved next under cover from the machine gun platoon. Lieutenant Wells's Third Platoon caught it hard, on the open sand, and began to take casualties. But the platoon rushed on and soon came up to the pillbox line. Several of the pillboxes had been knocked out and more damaged by the bombardments, but there were still plenty of Japanese soldiers in and around them. Marine Don Ruhl saw a satchel charge land, and jumped to cover it with his body, in order to protect others. He was blown apart, and another Medal of Honor was won.

In a trench up ahead, the Japanese seemed to be trying to organize a *banzai* charge, although such had been forbidden by General Kuribayashi. Men of the Third Platoon broke it up by lobbing grenades into the trench, and firing with BARS, two BAR men standing up alternately and firing into the trench, then the first man ducking back to reload while the other BAR went into action. The members of the squad threw so many grenades their fingers got sore, and then they ran out of grenades. One of the BAR men was shot dead, and the attack seemed to lose some impetus, but two more squads came up and renewed the firing. A light machine gun was brought up and put on the line, firing until its gunner was killed and the gun was knocked out.

A bunker ahead began spouting grenades, and the marines were all out of grenades. Rifle fire did not stop the grenades. Two men volunteered to go back for grenades, but both were killed on the way. The assault squad came up with demolition charges and a flamethrower. But the man with the satchel charge threw it and missed. The charge went off and rocked the area, but did not kill the Japanese in the bunker. The grenades began flying again.

The Japanese mortars began to find this position. Shells were coming very close, and an amphibious tractor coming up with supplies was hit. The mortars closed in on E company's Second Platoon and killed several men, when the rest of the assault squad came up with two flamethrowers. The mortars caused plenty of damage, and one shell burst wounded five men. By now the platoon had lost a third of its men in forty-five minutes. But the flamethrower men moved up, covered by the riflemen. One by one they approached the bunkers and pillboxes and fired into the apertures. Ammunition began to explode inside, and as they went from one to another the marines began to smell the odor of burning flesh.

The Most Dangerous Game 95

The tanks now arrived, brought in by the First Platoon, which had been held in reserve. The infantry men guided the tankers around mines, unexploded shells, and the dead and wounded.

With the tanks came the regimental 37mm guns and the 75mm half-tracks, and farther back the rocket trucks were sending rockets against the Japanese at the base of Suribachi. Several amphtracs came up with supplies and returned to the beach with loads of wounded.

The tanks and the infantry and the supporting weapons began to break up the interlocking fields of fire by the elimination of bunkers and pillboxes, and the effectiveness of the Japanese defense diminished.

During the afternoon Lieutenant Wells, who had suffered a number of minor wounds in the last two days, was still directing the attack of the Third Platoon of Easy Company, but finally he gave up and turned the platoon over to Platoon Sergeant Ernest Thomas and went to the rear for treatment.

A spotter plane had seen Japanese moving about among some trenches on the front of Easy Company and suggested that the Japanese were planning a *banzai* attack. The men of the company placed their machine guns in position to command those trenches and called for an air strike. The carrier planes hit the area, very enthusiastically, some of their attacks coming very close to the marine line. Then the Second Platoon made a charge of its own, and overran the Japanese trenches, killing several Japanese and chasing many others back up toward the base of the mountain.

At about three o'clock in the afternoon, Sergeant Thomas and a few men of the Third Platoon and one of the tanks moved up to the base of the mountain, the first marines to get there. Thomas jumped up on top of a bank at the edge of the mountain and waved his helmet.

But there was more to be done down there. The First Platoon faced a very large bunker with concrete walls four feet thick, guarding the slope of Mt. Suribachi. Inside were a field piece and a heavy machine gun. A tank came up, but did not do much damage to the big bunker. The bazooka man fired into the bunker and knocked out some chunks of concrete. The machine gun kept the marines careful, but they worked their way around to the flank and could hear the Japanese talking inside. They threw some grenades in through the ventilators, and after that the bunker was quiet. A flamethrower came up and hosed the interior with fire just for good measure.

This bunker's fall represented the first breach of the Japanese Suribachi defense, and Lieutenant Colonel Chandler Johnson was jubilant.

After Easy Company knocked out that bunker, they were moved around to the left, where the cliff fell down to the beach. One of the marines watched from the cliff and saw a machine gun firing on marines down by the water. As he was watching, a destroyer escort also saw the gun and started firing on it. The gun succumbed to the 40mm guns of the destroyer escort.

Late afternoon came, and the marines began to settle down for the night. Company E found itself cut off. The troops of the Second Battalion had pulled back, and several of the bunkers and pillboxes that the men of Company E had bypassed had now come to life and were manned by Japanese with machine guns.

E Company called for help, and two destroyers moved in and hit the slope above them with 40mm gunfire. The company moved out near the beach and set up their perimeter. They spent a restless night, hungry, without rations or much water.

So the marines buttoned up on the night of D + 2 and tried to get some rest for the resumption of the grueling fight that they knew would come the next day. They had suffered another thousand casualties, and they now held about a third of the island.

General Kuribayashi's report to Tokyo indicated that the attempt to push the marines off the island on the beaches had failed. The Japanese newspapers began to speculate on the day that the Allies would attack Japan itself. It was the first grim public recognition that the war was coming to the shores of Japan.

So far, the fleet had been largely on the attacking end, and had not had much opposition from the Japanese in the air. But on the morning of February 21, D + 2, thirty-two Japanese planes of a suicide unit took off from Katori airfield on Honshu Island,

The Most Dangerous Game 97

and headed for Iwo Jima. They stopped to refuel at Hachijo Jima. The unit was divided into five groups. Three groups each consisted of four fighters and four carrier bombers, and one group was made up of four torpedo bombers and one of four land-based torpedo bombers.

At about 4:30 on the afternoon of D + 2 the carrier *Saratoga* had just reached her operating area for the night, thirty-five miles northwest of Iwo Jima. Her job was to provide combat air patrol for the amphibious forces after they left the island for the night and moved out to sea. *Saratoga* was now a part of the task force's night carrier group which had been developed because of the Japanese *kamikaze* raids in the Philippines both at night and in the twilight hours.

When strange planes were seen by radar coming toward the carrier, at first they were judged to be American, from one of the other carriers. The *Saratoga* was then operating with most of her planes on board. But when the "bogeys" were reported seventy-five miles out, a half dozen fighters of the combat air patrol were sent to take a look. At ten minutes before five o'clock a pilot shouted "Tallyho," which meant he was attacking an enemy plane, and then announced that he had shot down two Zeros. Thus the men of the *Saratoga* knew that they were about to be attacked.

It was an ideal time for a *kamikaze* attack. The ceiling was low, about 3,500 feet, which favored the attackers and not the defenders. The *Saratoga* immediately went to high speed, and began catapulting fighters to join the defense. Just before five o'clock her antiaircraft guns began to fire, as a number of planes burst out of the clouds overhead. Two of them, which had been hit, struck the water alongside and bounded into the *Saratoga*, and their bombs went into the ship.

In the next three minutes, the level of excitement was beyond belief. The *Saratoga* had just launched fifteen planes, and two other fighters were on the catapults when a bomb exploded on the anchor windlass and knocked out much of the forward flight deck. A fourth attacker splashed alongside without doing any damage. A fifth plane, also in flames, made a flat turn and crashed into the port catapult. The sixth plane, also in flames, crashed a crane on the starboard side of the carrier. Parts landed on the gun galleries, and the rest went overboard.

As a ship, the *Saratoga* was still all right, but as a carrier she was in trouble. The power plant was unhurt, and the hangar deck fires were extinguished, but the flight deck was not able to take planes. The planes that had to land were directed to the various escort carriers.

Then, shortly before seven o'clock that night, as the *Saratoga* was getting back into fighting trim, parachute flares started falling around the carriers, and five more *kamikazes* attacked the *Saratoga*. Four were shot down outside the danger zone for the carrier, but the fifth, which came in quietly, was not seen, and dropped a bomb that exploded just above the flight deck and blew a 25-foot hole in the deck.

So the *Saratoga* had several wounds, but by shortly after eight o'clock that night she was recovering planes on the after flight deck. Still she was hard hit, and left the battle zone for Enewetak and then the west coast for major repairs. She lost forty-two planes that day in the fight, and had casualties of 123 killed and 192 men wounded.

The *kamikazes* were not finished for the night, either. The escort carrier *Bismarck Sea* caught the attention of some of the planes of Mitate Unit No. 2. One Japanese plane came in on her port bow, and a second came in on the starboard side, crashed the ship near the after elevator, and then dropped onto the hangar deck. This started gasoline fires, and then the bomb and torpedo stowage began to burn and exploded, blowing out the after end of the ship. A few minutes after seven o'clock that night, the captain ordered the ship abandoned. She burned and exploded for three hours, and then capsized and sank. More than two hundred of her 1,000-man crew were lost.

And the Japanese also attacked the escort carrier *Lunga Point*. Three torpedo planes came in and dropped torpedoes, all of which missed narrowly. But one of the planes then crashed into the island and skidded across the deck, then into the sea. A fourth plane was shot down. The *Lunga Point* had a narrow escape from disaster, but she was hurt only slightly and operations never stopped, nor was anyone hurt.

And the final ship hit that night by the Mitate Unit No. 2 was the cargo ship *Keokuk* which was crashed by a *kamikaze*. It killed seventeen men and wounded forty-four. Finally one more *kamikaze* crashed into LST 477, but did very little damage to the ship or her cargo of tanks.

Even so, this first effort from Japan of the newly-constituted *kamikaze* corps of the homeland navy had been very effective. Thirty-two planes had taken one major carrier out of action, sunk an escort carrier, damaged another, and damaged a cargo ship.

The Japanese reporting system was so imperfect that only the *Saratoga* attack was known. It was not until after the war ended that the Japanese learned they had sunk the *Bismarck Sea* that night. The reason the reporting was so fragmentary is that not a single pilot of the Mitate Unit No. 2 survived the attack.

On Iwo Jima on D + 3 there still wasn't much to do. The advance was stalled all along the line. As for the Scouts and Snipers, they were still waiting for action. They worked as litter bearers that day and that night. The big excitement was the moment that an artillery shell came over and hit the battalion aid station right in the middle. Four men were killed and ten were wounded. It was a bad day for the offensive on the northern segment of the island. By midmorning the weather had become so severe the carrier planes could not operate. The fresh Twenty-first Marines of the Third Division advanced only from 50 to 260 yards along their irregular front that day. Company F of the Second Battalion took so many casualties that it had to be taken out of the line. On the morning of D + 3, the Japanese defenders of Mt. Suribachi could look out and see the marines on the slopes of their mountain wherever there was space. The American ships and the American artillery on the land were firing, and the Japanese could tell that it would not be long before a final attack was made up the slopes.

Colonel Kanehiko Atsuchi, the commander of the garrison, requested permission from General Kuribayashi to stage a *banzai* attack rather than waiting mutely for the end to come to them. General Kuribayashi refused permission. He wanted organized resistance to continue as long as possible.

All three battalions of the Twenty-eighth Marines tightened up their lines and consolidated their gains. The Third Battalion had a little way to go to reach the base, and they made it. There was some hand-to-hand fighting as Japanese left behind made dashes for the caves on the mountain. A marine officer who spoke Japanese went forward with a loudspeaker calling on the Japanese to surrender, but his efforts were ignored. Only a few prisoners were taken, most of them badly wounded. By the end of the day, the marines held the base all around the mountain. The next job was to climb to the top, and that would come on D + 4. By the night of D + 3 the Twenty-eighth Marines had lost sixteen officers and nearly 300 men.

On the night of D + 3, the beaches were still jammed up. The landing vessels unloaded all night long. That night the carriers of Task Force Fifty-eight left Iwo Jima. The plan for the assault had envisaged its completion in about four days, and it had been expected that the job of Task Force Fifty-eight in air support of the ground forces would be finished, so they were scheduled to make another attack on Japan and then hit Okinawa, to soften it up for the landings.

On the morning of D + 4 the Twenty-eighth Marines moved to take Mt. Suribachi. The only practicable way up the mountain was on the northeast slope, which meant that the brunt of the attack would be borne by Lieutenant Colonel Johnson's Second Battalion.

Up north, the Twenty-fourth's Scout-Sniper Platoon was still waiting for its orders. That day they worked as Graves Registration, bringing in the bodies of dead marines for identification and marking. To get the bodies, they had to go up under mortar and artillery fire. They waited some more. Then a Japanese shell came in and hit an ammunition dump a hundred yards from the command post. Several men were wounded, including one of the Scout-Snipers, who got it in the arm.

That morning they were finally called. Lieutenant William Holder and two marines of the platoon went ahead to scout the course for the Second Battalion to follow up the ridge. The ledges ahead were a broken area of traps, holes, and caves. Some of the concrete pillboxes were shattered from the naval gunfire, but one never knew whether or not some Japanese might still be in there. It seemed that every pile of sand concealed a sniper, a machine gun, or a mortar.

K Company dug in at the bottom of the first rise, and the Scout-Sniper Platoon job for the rest of that day was to provide security for the command post and the mortar section. That meant searching the area for caves and holes and sealing them up. If they came to a cave with only one entrance, they sealed it with a demolition charge. If it had two entrances, marines stood by each entrance and simultaneously threw in grenades. They moved around in a skirmish line, close to the ground. Several times they were driven back to cover by mortar attacks.

By evening, they had done a day's work, but Company K still wasn't satisfied, so Lieutenant Holder led out a mopping-up squad of five men. When they came back, they had new orders. The area between Company K of the Third Battalion and Company E of the Second Battalion had suffered a gap by losses. The Scout-Sniper Platoon would now have to serve as riflemen for the night.

So they went up in two squads abreast. The Japanese saw them coming and opened fire. They moved ahead for 150 yards. One man was wounded and headed back to the evacuation station.

They reached some abandoned Japanese foxholes and dug in there. They were joined by a machine gun section, and they set up a machine gun on each end of the position, with three men in a foxhole between.

Three men were on rear guard watch.

At nine o'clock, the man on front watch heard Japanese voices. First he thought he was imagining it, but then he heard them again. He fired forty rounds with his tommygun and the voices ceased.

The three-man rear guard suddenly heard something suspicious, and then they saw a group of Japanese coming at the them through the scrub. They began firing, and some of the shapes fell. The others ran, parallel to the lines. Then everyone was throwing grenades, and rocks, gravel, and pieces of Japanese bodies flew through the air.

These were the Japanese they saw. Most of the Japanese they did not see, except in flashes.

In the morning, the line moved ahead after a barrage laid down by three halftracks mounting 75mm guns and 81mm mortars hitting the Japanese positions ahead. But when the line moved, the fire from the Japanese machine guns seemed just as heavy as before, and the snipers just as accurate.

The marines came to the edge of a brown cliff. About a hundred yards from this point, the Japanese laid down a fierce hail of fire from a position on that hill.

Lieutenant Holder was wounded, as was another man next to him. A sergeant took over the platoon. Their machine gun on the left was hit by a mortar round and knocked out. Then another mortar shell hit the machine gun on the right flank, and it was gone. One by one the men of the platoon were falling, dead and wounded. The sergeant got the men together around a large hole made by some big gun, and they waited. They were told they would resume the attack at one thirty in the afternoon. While they waited, they tried to recover the right hand machine gun. The men using it had been killed, but someone said he thought the gun was still workable. There was a 50-yard gap in the line, and the sergeant did not have enough men to fill it. There had been about twenty men there not long ago. Now there were four. Another hour went by and somebody counted the men in the platoon. Of the platoon of thirty, nine men were left in the line.

CHAPTER THIRTEEN

The Capture of Mt. Suribachi

It was still raining. A moving fog hung over Mt. Suribachi that morning. The fog swirled around the rim of the crater and gathered in the cracks and gulleys of the mountain.

Very early in the morning, a four-man patrol from the Twenty-eighth Marines' F Company went up Mt. Suribachi. They returned to report that many Japanese were still in their defensive positions on the mountain. On the basis of their report, Lieutenant Colonel Johnson made his attack plan. He assembled a forty-man combat patrol from the Third Platoon of E Company and battalion headquarters. Lieutenant Harold Schrier, the executive officer of Company E, was put in command.

There were actually about 900 Japanese left in the caves and defenses of Suribachi. Colonel Atsuchi was still smarting from General Kuribayashi's response to the request to make a *banzai* charge against the enemy. He had said absolutely no, and added an acid comment.

"I had imagined the the first airfield would be overrun quickly, but what has happened to cause Mt. Suribachi to fall in only three days?"

But General Kuribayashi was not the only one having a frustrating time. Colonel Harry Liversedge's command post for the Twenty-eighth Marines had been established at the front of the volcano, and at daylight a Japanese artillery shell from the north made a direct hit, killing the regimental surgeon.

All three battalions of the Twenty-eighth Marines were to be involved in the capture of Suribachi, but Easy Company, on the southeast side of the base of the mountain, was in the best position for the actual assault on the top. The company, having been isolated by the rapid movement of the late afternoon on the day before, had gotten through the night without much trouble, helped by American destroyers, which laid down fire on the mountainside. Colonel Atsuchi's men had carried out several missions of infiltration to harry the Americans, but these had been on the northern and western sides of the island. By dawn, the Japanese had vanished from the pillboxes, cleaned out by the company on its afternoon assault and then later reoccupied from the caves where they had taken refuge. Several rockslides caused by the destroyer fire had also helped clean up that side of the mountain. The Easy Company wounded were taken off by life raft, and some ammunition and rations were brought in. The company's contact with the other units of the battalion was reestablished.

Lieutenant Colonel Johnson told the assault patrol that they would take the American flag that had come ashore on D Day to be raised on Mt. Suribachi. They were to take the height, put up the flag to show that they had taken it, and hold the position there.

The rain continued, but let up long enough for an air strike. Most of the bombs fell on the mountainside, but one "friendly" bomb dropped right in the middle of Company E, knocking one man out of the hole which he was digging.

The rain started in again, and the fighting began. Because the men of the Third Battalion had not reached the base of the mountain the day before, they had to do the hardest fighting to get there, while the other two battalions consolidated their positions and more or less waited.

Much of the fighting was hand-to-hand. Japanese soldiers would suddenly dart from cover to make an attack. One marine was charged by an officer swinging a *samurai* sword. He grabbed the sword by the blade, wrung it free, and killed the officer with it, suffering two badly cut hands in the process, but winning his own *samurai* sword the hard way.

The marines used every weapon: artillery, mortars, machine guns, rifles, BARS, tanks, and grenades. They also used psychological warfare, dropping leaflets and using a loudspeaker system to address the Japanese and try to persuade them to surrender. But the Japanese discipline was very good, and only one man surrendered. He was found wounded and almost completely buried at the bottom of a shell hole. Another Japanese in a shell hole pretended to be dead. Two marines dropped into the shell hole and saw this half-buried man, with a pistol in his right hand and a *samurai* sword near its left hand. They skirted the shell hole and were nearly past it, when one marine suddenly turned and fired at the body. The other marine asked why. "His eyes followed us all around the shell hole," said the first marine.

By the end of the day Colonel Liversedge's men had consolidated their positions around the base of the mountain. Patrols from the First and the Second Battalions met at the water's edge in the rear of Suribachi and found the lower slopes had been largely cleared of Japanese. The next day they would go to the top, the colonel said.

February 23 dawned clear as the sun came up. At about eight o'clock Lieutenant Schrier assembled the attack patrol. They reported to the battalion command post, and Lieutenant Colonel Johnson gave them the flag. The men took an extra supply of cartridges, grenades, demolition charges, and flamethrower fuel. They filled their canteens and were joined here by a radio man, two teams of stretcher bearers, and photographer, Staff Sergeant Louis Lowery of *Leatherneck*, the marine magazine. As they looked at the steep slope of Mt. Suribachi, the marines speculated on the two sets of stretcher bearers. They might need a lot more than that, but the colonel was very matter-of-fact about the mission. The morning patrols had not encountered a lot of trouble, and so the later one would not, he said. Then he got on the telephone to regiment and asked that all fire be withheld from the slope of Suribachi, and that the navy be notified to keep its big guns silent.

The marines moved out then in an irregular column, heading for the base of the volcano. They passed dead marines, a marine howitzer that had taken a direct hit from an enemy shell, dead Japanese, and broken up pillboxes. The route grew steeper, and the lieutenant sent out flankers to guard against surprise. The men had more than the usual weight of ammunition and supplies, and the going was slow. It was only five hundred feet, but it seemed like much more. In some places the patrol from the Second Battalion had to go up the gullies on hands and knees. So they went up the north face of the mountain walking, stumbling, and crawling. There were trails up, but the marines assumed that these had been mined, and stayed well away from them. At ten o'clock, as the patrol neared the top, the men spread out around the rim of the crater for a break, while Lieutenant Schrier took a look. They could see several battered gun emplacements and some cave entrances, but they saw no Japanese. Lieutenant Schrier signalled, and they dashed over the rim, seven of them: Snyder, Keller, Robeson, Schrier, Charlo, and Rozek and Leader. There was nothing on the other side but a deep lava pit.

Half the patrol stayed at the rim of the crater and the other half moved down inside. What they needed was a flagpole. They began looking in the debris of the fighting for something that would do.

Marine Harold Keller made contact with the enemy. He came to a ridge, and on the other side was a deep hole. He looked down into it and a Japanese soldier began coming up, his back to Keller. The marine fired three times from the hip, and the Japanese dropped out of sight. But then several hitherto quiet caves began to shoot out grenades. The marines replied with grenades. The Japanese threw some of them back out of the caves.

Marines Robert Leader and Leo Rozek found the flagpole, a long piece of pipe that seemed to be part of the remnants of a raincatch. They passed it up to the summit of Mt. Suribachi. Up at the top were Lieutenant Schrier and three other marines. Platoon Sergeant Ernest Thomas fired a shot through the pipe near the top and the men laced the flag on to their flagpole. A

The Capture of Mt. Suribachi   107

10:20, they began to plant the pole, so that the Stars and Stripes could fly over Iwo Jima for the first time. Photographer Lowery took a picture of the flag raising and it was seen all over the island.

So the Marines had captured Mt. Suribachi. It had been 10:35 when Lieutenant Schrier, Platoon Sergeant Ernest Thomas, Sergeant Henry Hanson, Corporal Charles Lindberg, and Private First Class James Michaelis raised the flag, as Private First Class James Robeson stood guard with a BAR. A Japanese threw a grenade and Robeson shot him down. Another Japanese grabbed the body by the feet and pulled it back into the cave. Still another Japanese came rushing up, wielding a *samurai* sword. Marine Snyder advanced on this officer with his .45 automatic, but the pistol misfired. He scrambled to get out of the way as his fellow marines shot the officer.

These Japanese had come out of a big cave, and the marines headed toward it. More grenades came flying out of caves, and the marines replied with grenades. Photographer Lowery neared the entrance to the cave with his camera. He heard a rapping noise, which he recognized as a Japanese arming a grenade by tapping it on his helmet, and then the grenade came out of the cave. He jumped for safety and ran fifty feet. The grenade exploded, but he was out of range. He stumbled and fell and broke his camera, but his film of the flag raising was saved.

Other marines now came up and worked over the caves around the summit. The big cave was closed up by blowing the entrances with grenades, and an estimated 150 Japanese were sealed up in it.

When the patrol went back down to battalion headquarters, Lieutenant Colonel Johnson decided that they ought to get another flag, so they could keep this flag as the battalion's souvenir. So he sent a lieutenant down to the beach to find a big flag. The lieutenant searched around. He boarded LST 779 and spoke to the LST's communications officer, Ensign Alan Wood, who happened to have a flag eight feet long and four feet wide, which he had found at a naval salvage depot in Pearl Harbor. So the lieutenant accomplished his mission. He took

108 IWO JIMA

the flag back to the battalion command post, and Lieutenant Colonel Johnson sent it up the mountain with orders that it be put up in place of the little flag.

So marines were put to searching around for a new flagpole for the bigger flag and did find a large long piece of pipe.

It was all done over again. The little flag was lowered, and at the same moment the big flag was raised.

The new flag raisers were Marines Mike Strand, Rent Gagnon, Ira Hayes, G. Block, and Franklin Sousley, and Navy Corpsman John Bradley. Several photographers had come up to the summit by this time, including Joe Rosenthal, a photographer for the Associated Press. All the photographers took the picture of the lowering of the first flag and the raising of the second, but Rosenthal got a particularly dramatic shot, with a stiff wind whipping the flag as it was raised. The Associated Press served many American newspapers, which received the photograph a few days later, while the fighting was still going on at Iwo Jima. So this second flag raising provided what became the best known picture of the Pacific War, and epitomized the whole struggle of Americans to defeat the Japanese in the Far East.

Down below, the marines on the beachhead cheered as they saw the flag run up. Once the flag was raised, Lieutenant Schrier called the men to get going. "We haven't time to waste around here," he said. "Let's get back to work."

Down below them other marines of the Second Battalion were clearing the Japanese from the mountain, fighting their way up. One company was fighting about two hundred Japanese in a tangle of caves which were hidden by underbrush. Private First Class Harold Benedict grabbed the only flamethrower left in the company and began dousing the brush, hitting the cave openings, to get the attack going. He did this for five hours under fire most of the time, without getting hurt.

By the end of the day most of the Japanese on Suribachi were dead. The assault had cost the Twenty-eighth Marines nearly 900 casualties. Seven officers and two hundred men had been killed. The marines counted more than 1,200 dead Japanese but these did not represent a true count. Many more Japanese had been sealed in caves and blockhouses. More than a thousand Japanese emplacements of various kinds were destroyed. That afternoon Father Suter came up to the top of Mt. Suribachi. Several marines helped him build an altar of rocks beneath the flag and he said mass there.

The marines of the Twenty-eighth Regiment continued to mop up for two more days and then stayed in reserve for five days picking off Japanese stragglers. Engineers completed the destruction of 165 concrete pillboxes and blockhouses. They had blasted away fifteen bunkers and had buried or detonated thousands of rounds of ammunition and landmines. They had sealed up two hundred caves. They evacuated the wounded, and the engineers built roads around the crater.

A week after the landing, Mt. Suribachi was an artillery spotting point for the ships off shore and the marine artillery on the shore. Secretary of the Navy James V. Forrestal arrived at Iwo Jima and came to the Suribachi area to walk on the shore. General Smith wanted to climb the mountain, but was told that the terrain was too rugged. They walked around the shore, and Secretary Forrestal saw a shell hit a hundred yards from the men, killing and wounding twenty.

They saw the flag, and knew the story, and Forrestal remarked to General Smith:

"Holland, the raising of that flag means a Marine Corps for the next five hundred years."

CHAPTER FOURTEEN

The Medics

On Iwo Jima, the doctors and corpsmen came in with the first waves of marines. Each battalion had its own surgeon, thirteen navy corpsmen, and twenty stretcher bearers. The marines landed and the medics looked around for a little shelter in which to put up an aid station. They discovered shelter was hard to find on the beaches of Iwo Jima. As the marines moved, so did the aid station. They were never more than about two hundred yards from the action.

When a marine was hit, a corpsman would get to him as soon as possible, douse the wound with sulfa, stop the bleeding if he could, give morphine to dull the pain, and get the wounded man to the aid station. That meant four stretcher bearers to carry the wounded man, often with gunfire crackling around.

At the aid station the doctor would make a diagnosis and give what treatment he could. Then the marine's jacket was tagged and he was sent back to the beach and to a ship as quickly as possible. In the first few days, the progress was very slow, because of the debris on the beaches and the shortage of transportation. In the early days of the fighting, litter bearers were a high casualty group. One case illustrates. A corporal was badly hit in the fight and his legs were broken. A four-man litter team was carrying him across the runway of Airfield No. 1 when a shell landed nearby. The wounded man dived off the stretcher into a shell hole and was not hurt. Two of the litter bearers were killed and the other two badly wounded by the shellburst.

Once a man got to the shore, and aboard a boat, and to a ship, his chances of survival were very good. It was the in-between time that resulted in the loss of many men, through inattention and lack of care at crucial moments.

In the planning, the Fourth and Fifth Divisions hospitals were scheduled to be operating ashore by the afternoon of D + 2. But it was D + 4 before the Fourth Division's hospital was in operation, and later for the Fifth. In the meantime, the battalion surgeons worked in shell holes and under tarpaulins, anywhere they could find what looked like shelter from the storm of war. In midmorning of D + 4, the Fourth Division hospital was operating in a revetment on the eastern edge of Airfield No. 1. Bulldozers had carved out an embankment in the cliff, but the area was still wide open to shelling. The medics worked in two long green tents and six small ones, with eight operating tables, an X-ray machine and a refrigerator for drugs, plasma, and blood. The power was provided by generators that sputtered and sometimes quit, and then emergency battery lights supplied the lighting. One tent was a recovery ward with eighty cots.

Iwo Jima was notable because it was the first time in the Pacific that whole blood became available on the battlefield.

During the first two days, no one had time to worry about the dead. There was no place to bury them, and the enemy barrage and mortar fire was so heavy that nothing could be done. But at the end of D + 1, the dead became a morale factor. Correspondent Sherrod had reported seeing piles of arms and legs and intestines strung out on the sand. Those sights were unnerving to marines coming in, so the Graves Registration units were put to work in the Fourth and Fifth Division areas. Two hundred yards inland from Beach Red, where the black sandy terraces sloped down from the hillside, they located the burial grounds. Ultimately there would be three of them, one near Suribachi, and the other two side by side near the north-south runway of Airfield No. 1. First the gravediggers had to get the land mines and the dug shells out of the area.

Many line marines were pressed into service to clear away the bodies. Bodies and parts of bodies were placed on ponchos on stretchers. Then they were gone over for identification, and sometimes fingerprints pulled and dental charts made. But there were too many bodies and too little time for individual attention. Bulldozers cut trenches eight feet deep and thirty yards long and the bodies were placed in the long lines. Each grave was listed on a master location chart with vital information about the dead. Prepainted wooden crosses and markers were put together and stenciled with the men's names. But there were still many burials of bodies marked "Unknown."

A problem arose with the Japanese dead. If unburied they posed a threat to public health, and the stink and sight of the blasted bodies was repugnant to everyone. When enemy bodies were found in a cluster, bulldozers heaped earth over them, but there were not many of these, because General Kuribayashi's orders to conceal the dead were too well followed. Whenever possible the Japanese recovered bodies and hid them in caves. Thus the caves of Iwo Jima became an enormous cemetery, for the marines sealed many Japanese in, and many killed themselves in the caves. The wounded died in the underground hospitals.

At one point in the battle, a patrol of scouts and snipers found their way into a cave complex used as a hospital and then as a crematorium. They saw dead enemy troops lining the passageways, and as they went deeper, they found that an officer and eleven wounded men were still alive at the end. They wanted some time to decide whether to commit suicide or surrender. The Americans waited an hour, and finally the men came out. The officer had been shot in both legs and was carried on a stretcher by four of the men. The others hobbled out alone. They bowed and the officer asked to keep his saber. The American officer gave permission. The patrol took them out and sealed up the entrance to the cave, thus entombing another two hundred Japanese dead in the caves of Iwo Jima.

CHAPTER FIFTEEN

The Main Attack

By February 23, the main line of the American attack had moved about two miles from Suribachi, stretching across the island from east to west. Between the front and the north tip of the island it was another two miles, and in these two miles were the heart and sinews of General Kuribayashi's defenses. The island had the look of a moonscape, gray and cratered, with no vegetation to show that any life existed. The marines faced barren prairie without grass, twisting ravines, cliffs dropping into gullies, and here and there some sticks of brushwood.

In the center, at the second airport, Colonel Ikeda commanded the defenses. And the Twenty-first Marines of the Third Marine Division were trying to break through. They tried all day and made virtually no gains at all, though they tried bravely. While waiting to attack, one platoon saw the raising of the flag on Mt. Suribachi and became so invigorated that they got up and walked forward across the airstrip. But the fire increased as they did so, and men began to drop. In the end the gallant effort failed, and the Twenty-first Marines were right back where they had started the day.

On the right the Fourth Marine Division had made some gains that day, 100 to 300 yards. And that was all.

The two miles of barren ground that lay between Suribachi and the front were still honeycombed with Japanese defenses that had been bypassed. That night of February 23, a Japanese battalion commander reported that his headquarters bunker and its cave were now inside the American lines, and under attack by flamethrowers and grenades, and that he had lost contact with many pillboxes.

"Nevertheless the fighting spirit of all men and officers is high. We shall continue to inflict as much damage as possible upon the enemy until we are all annihilated. We pray for final victory and the safety of our country."

Admiral Ichimaru, the naval commander of the island, radioed to Combined Fleet headquarters that the real struggle for Iwo Jima was yet to come, and that he and his men would defend the island to the death, every man fulfilling his duty. On the night of the twenty-third, the marines on Suribachi were kept awake by the sound of explosions within the mountain. These were the explosions of grenades, as trapped Japanese killed themselves. But a number of Japanese that night made their way out of the caves down the mountain and across the two miles of newly captured marine territory to join their comrades on the other side. They were not always well received. A navy lieutenant and three of his men who had made the trip safely, came to the headquarters of Naval Captain Samaji Inouye and the lieutenant reported that Suribachi had fallen to the marines.

The captain erupted in fury. He called the lieutenant a coward and invoked shame on him for being alive when Suribachi had fallen. He drew his *samurai* sword and told the lieutenant he would execute him personally for his misbehavior. The lieutenant bent his head to receive the blow, but the captain's men took his sword away from him and finally calmed him down while the lieutenant and his men went off to have their wounds treated.

This was a sample of the attitude of the navy contingent on Iwo Jima, which was contemptuous of the army's attitude of preservation of lives until the last. The navy men wanted to make *banzai* charges and mow down the enemy, giving no consideration to how long they would last thus. Kuribayashi steadfastly ignored Admiral Ichimaru's complaints, and the admiral made them to Tokyo, where they received some sympathy but no action.

That night of February 23, there was some of the usual infiltration tactics, but not too much.

On the morning of February 24, D + 5, the main thrust of the marines was against Colonel Ikeda's defense on the second airfield. This was the crucial point, and the movement of the troops on right and left depended on success here. The Twenty-first Marines formed up, with the Second Battalion on the left and the Third Battalion on the right. The Third Battalion had been in reserve in the early fighting, while the First Battalion had exhausted itself and been decimated. Lieutenant Colonel Wendell DuPlantis, the commander of the battalion, told his men they had to take that airfield. So the word went down to the platoons and squads.

The attack was to have the strongest combination of fire and bombardment that could be put together, and the tanks from all three marine divisions had been brought in to assemble behind the center. The battleship *Idaho* began the firing at eight o'clock in the morning with her fourteen-inch guns. She was joined in the firing by the cruiser *Pensacola*. Their target was a fortified ridge north of the airfield, a thousand yards from the line occupied by the Third Battalion. But this was their target, too, and they had to reach it, take it, and hold it to achieve the breakthrough that was expected.

The artillery began firing at 8:45. Fifteen minutes later, it stopped to allow the carrier planes a chance to get into action. They bombed and strafed and used napalm.

Now the concentration of tanks started forward along two taxiways of the airfield. But the Japanese had expected this, and they had placed antitank mines and had the ground zeroed in for their artillery and mortars. The leading tank in the western lane hit a mine and was disabled. Another tank moved around it and struck a buried aerial torpedo and was blown up. Other tanks behind were stopped by antitank fire, and in the other lane the mines were the chief menace. The tank attack bogged down.

The infantry was dependent on the tanks for support across the long open space of the airfield, and so now the whole attack bogged down. But an order came to start off without the tanks, and so Company I and Company K moved out abreast, their front about 400 yards wide. They were about 800 yards south of the center of the airfield where the runways crossed, and the ridge was on the other side.

Machine guns were covering their advance by firing, and other machine guns were moving up with the marines. Behind, the mortars were trying to soften up the defenses with a barrage of their own.

But as the marines moved they met heavy fire from rifles, machine guns, and mortars.

Company K and Company I kept moving. They took out some of the pillboxes, but their orders were to keep on going and let someone else do the mopping up. They were heading for that ridge line. Captain Rodney Heinze, commander of K Company, was wounded by a Japanese grenade, and First Lieutenant Raoul J. Archambault took over the company. Then Captain Clayton Rockmore, the commander of I Company, was killed by a Japanese bullet. Three platoon commanders were shot down in short order, but non-coms took over and the attack went on.

By 11:45 a handful of marines had reached the northern edge of the airstrip. First Lieutenant Dominic Grossi led his platoon across the strip, but by this time only a squad of a dozen men were left in the platoon. Another platoon, now down to the same size, came up, and together they started up the last fifty yards of the brush. But they were hit by misplaced friendly artillery fire, and they were driven off the slope. They came down and started up again, this time to be driven back by the Japanese. The marines started a third attack but it, too, failed to reach the top. The Japanese enfilading fire made the difference. The marines picked up their wounded and fell back to consolidate with the other marine forces.

At 1:30 in the afternoon, after another naval, air, and artillery barrage, the two assault companies resumed the attack. Lieutenant Archambault led K Company until it reached the foot of the hill again. When all the men arrived, there were fewer than 200 of them. But they started up the hill. When they got almost to the top, the Japanese charged over from the other side, and the fight developed into a hand-to-hand combat, some men fighting with entrenching tools, some with rifles, some with grenades, and some with bayonet or combat knife. The fight did not last long. In about ten minutes the marines triumphed and had control of the ridge, while about fifty Japanese dead lay near the top.

I Company came up, and so did several tanks.

On the Twenty-sixth Marine front, progress was also made this day. One battalion moved about 800 yards, but on the west coast the 127th Marines were slowed by the Japanese defense of a valley dominated by a ridge full of caves and bunkers. In the valley itself the Japanese had built many pillboxes which were manned vigorously.

On the right the Fourth Division was still unable to move in the cliff area by the boat basin, but part of the Twenty-fourth Marines, who had worked their way inland, began to move toward a key point called Charlie Dog Ridge, at the southeastern edge of the No. 2 Airfield. Late in the afternoon the Third Battalion of the Twenty-fourth Marines took their objective.

The casualties were now up to 7,758, with the Fourth Division's casualty figure the highest. Its combat efficiency that night was measured at 60 percent. But that was not much worse than the rest of the divisions. Still, that night the marines were encouraged, because significant progress was being made in the drive up the island after those first stalled days.

What was called "the terrible two weeks" began on Sunday morning, the sixth day.

Now the capture of Mt. Suribachi and the territory just north of it seemed to have been the easy part of the battle. The only way to capture the remaining two-thirds of the island was to occupy the high ground in the middle. On the sides, east and west, the ground broke and ran down to the shore in sharp gullies, canyons, and cliffs. The attempts up by the old quarry had shown how expensive the warfare could be there. The shelling of the cliffs and caves had turned the mountainsides into waste areas of broken stone and debris.

On the west coast of Iwo Jima, the Fifth Division was faced with a fight for one ridge after another. The Japanese would have to be driven from the high ground in the center.

On the east, the Fourth Marine Division faced an even more difficult problem. The field on which they had to advance had been stripped of all its natural cover by the bombardments. Where once oak trees had grown, now there was only tangled brush, sharp broken rock, and gullies running to the sea. They faced here a central point in the Japanese defenses, built around the second highest point on the island, Hill 382.

Major General Graves B. Erskine, the commander of the Third Marine Division, had taken over control of all his troops, and the Ninth Marine regiment was in the line, with the Twenty-first Marines back for a little rest. The artillery of the corps, the Fourth Division, and the Fifth Division, were on the island, and the Third Division artillery was landing. The drive would now be up the center.

On the sixth day, a battleship and two cruisers opened the artillery assault, firing for twenty minutes. The marine artillery followed with 1,200 rounds across the front, and the carrier planes with 500-pound bombs came after that.

At 9:30, just after the air strike, the marines moved out. And once more they were shown the strength of the Japanese defenses. All that steel and explosive that had been rained on the Japanese lines had not diminished the effectiveness of their weapons. Again it would be a question of the infantry and the tanks and the flamethrowers routing out the enemy, one position after another.

As noted, General Smith had hoped to use only one regiment of the Third Marine Division at Iwo Jima, but now the Ninth Marines were in action along with the Twenty-first Marines in the center of the island. Smith was still holding the Third Marines, the last regiment left free, and hoping not to have to use them, because he wanted fresh troops for the coming invasion of Okinawa.

Another indication of progress was the beginning of reconstruction of the Airfield No. 1. It began with an inch-by-inch search for land mines and unexploded ammunition. The Seabees also put on a detailed search for shrapnel which would cut up the tires of landing aircraft. And the Twentieth Air Force in the Marianas could hardly wait for these fields to become operational, in order to provide fighter protection for their raids on Japan and to give them an emergency landing base halfway between the enemy targets and home.

The commanders of all three marine divisions were ashore, and so was General Harry Schmidt, the corps commander. More than 50,000 marines were ashore, and the shore and supply organizations were getting under control. The southern third of the island was one great beehive of supply activity. Roads were being built inland, and dumps were becoming depots. Men were putting up telephone poles to raise the phone lines off the sand, and the makeshift medical facilities were being replaced by field hospitals. The bulldozers and other earth-moving equipment were creating sheltered positions for command posts and aid stations.

That day, the casualties began to move to the beach and out to the ships with more regularity and speed. Nine ships left for Guam carrying 1,500 men wounded in the fighting of the early days.

The marines straightened out their front. The Fifth Division simply held, because it had gotten out in front of the others. The Third Division had to move up four hundred yards to get even, and this was to be done by the Ninth Marines, since the Twenty-first Marines had done the heavy fighting the day before.

The Fourth Division was facing the defenses of Major General Sadasue Senda, commander of the Second Mixed Brigade. His defense system was so powerful and well integrated that it became known as "The Meatgrinder" as the campaign went on. The defense was built around Hill 382, a bowl below it called the Amphitheater, a rise called Turkey Knob, and the existing village of Minami, whose buildings had been smashed up by the bombardments before and during the first days of the invasion, but whose deep fortifications were almost intact.

The defenses on the east coast of the island continued to be very strong and to hold back the other elements of the Fourth Division. The Twenty-fourth Marines had tried to go ahead, but had not been able to advance more than a quarter of a mile in any sector.

That morning of February 24, the men of the Third Division began the attack on the airport defenses, after an artillery preparation. Twenty tanks of the Third Tank Battalion headed forward, and the Japanese antitank defenses opened up on them with 150 mortars, five-inch guns, antitank guns, antiaircraftguns depressed to be antitank guns, and mines everywhere.

"They knocked hell out of us for a while," said Major Holly Evans, the commander of the tank unit. Three leading tanks were hit, one by one, and the last two burst into flame and their crews came tumbling out of the hatches. Corporal William Adamson, who jumped out of one of the stricken tanks, saw the antitank gun that was doing the damage, and started to go up to the first tank to point it out. He was hit by machine gun fire, and had to stop to take care of a wound in the leg, but he crawled up to the first tank and pointed out the antitank gun. The tankers disposed of it with their 75mm cannon.

Corporal Adamson then found four machine gun nests scattered in the rocks and pointed them out. The tankers turned their 75mm gun on the machine guns, one by one, and knocked them out. The Japanese tried to bring up a satchel charge, but the tank machine gun took care of the soldier with the charge. A platoon of Japanese then fled into a trench, and headed up toward the tank, intending to attack. But again Corporal Adamson spotted the movement, and the tank chewed up the trench with the 75mm gun. About half the Japanese platoon were killed and the others scattered, disorganized.

The tanks had a rough day. Before the day was over Major Evans's tanks were knocked out of action at such a rate that he had lost half his strength. But the result was that the Third Division troops took a firm hold in the high ground north of the airfield, which they held at the end of the day, except for a strip at the northeast.

The First Battalion of the Ninth Marines fought for five hours and advanced 100 yards to the foot of the hill called Hill Peter. The Second and Third battalions made better progress and by nightfall the line was north of Airfield No. 2, except at the right tip.

The Fourth Division's Twenty-third and Twenty-fourth regiments moved into The Meatgrinder, which lived up into its name. They had the artillery, the naval gunfire, the mortar boats offshore, and the landing craft with rockets, firing up the draws. They had carrier plane support. They tried to get over the rubble with tanks, failed, and sent them around through the Third Division area. They had armored bulldozers to clear the roads. They fought all day long, and by night they had gone forward an average of a hundred yards.

The Fifth Division had to wait for the others to come up, but they still took nearly 200 casualties that day from mortar and artillery fire. In spite of the victories in those first five days, there was no safe place on Iwo Jima. But that applied to the Japanese as well as to the Americans, if the Japanese ventured out into the open. In the afternoon of the sixth day, against the advice of their infantry commander, two Japanese heavy artillery batteries decided to move north. They were spotted by a plane at three o'clock that afternoon and the Fifth Division's artillery was given the job of routing them. The artillerymen fired 600 rounds, destroyed three Japanese artillery pieces, and set an ammunition dump ablaze. After that day, no more Japanese artillery moved during the daylight hours.

On the southern beaches, the invasion proceeded more nearly to plan. Hospitals continued to go up and roads were built. The Fifth Division engineers opened a water distillation plant on the west coast. They drove the pipes into the natural hot springs of the mountainside, and the water came out so hot it had to be cooled by running lines through the sea. From now on, in this rear area some men would get showers.

The Seabees finished repairing the north-south runway of Airfield No. 1 by nightfall. A strip 1,500 feet long and 150 feet wide was ready and cleared of all obstructions. A plane came in from the Marianas and delivered some airmail. The Iwo Jima campaign was supposed to have been won in three or four days, but nobody mentioned that now. The second week began on Monday morning, February 26, and nobody noticed.

122 IWO JIMA

In a week of fighting the marines had now captured 40 percent of the island, and the casualty figures was up well over 8,000. It was not at all the sort of battle that anyone had expected for this little piece of rock.

The Fifth Division made about 300 yards that day, and the Twenty-sixth Marines captured the last of the Japanese water wells on the island. Twenty of the amphibious tractors with 75mm guns were busy that day, moving off the west coast and firing their 75s up the canyons. They claimed at last three enemy strong points.

On February 26, which was D + 7, the Third Division and the Fifth Division launched a new offensive in the center and left of the line. The Third Division captured two important prominences, Hill Peter and Hill Oboe, which lay north of the No. 2 Airfield. The Fifth Division fought its way 700 yards and reached the approaches to Hill 362 A.

But the key was The Meatgrinder, and the high point of Hill 382. The Fourth Division continued to pound away at these defenses. On February 26, elements of the Twenty-third Marines went back into the line and fought around Turkey Knob and the Amphitheater. Around the East Boat Basin they wiped out a band of snipers and now general unloading began on the Fourth Division beaches.

The Third Battalion of the Twenty-third Marines attacked Hill 382 again. Private First Class Douglas T. Jacobson, took a bazooka up that hill and knocked out sixteen positions, killing 75 Japanese. For this he was later awarded the Medal of Honor.

In the afternoon, two little spotter planes landed on Airfield No. 1. Soon they would begin working regularly from the airfield to ferret out the Japanese. Several platoons of the Third Battalion managed to climb the first ridge of Hill 382, but as they reached the summit they were hit by heavy, coordinated Japanese fire from front, sides, and rear. Machine guns, mortars, and air rifles all began firing at once.

Some of the fire was originating from a large blockhouse on Turkey Knob, 500 yards to the right. Those marines who had made it to the top were now pinned down for the next eight hours. They had good cover, but the attack was unceasing, and it was joined by some grenade throwers on the other side of the ridge, who lobbed grenades at the marines, causing a number of casualties. One platoon of Company C lost half its men here, and other platoons were almost as badly hit.

Company I was also pinned down. First Lieutenant Harcourt E. Waller, Jr., could see a Japanese command post in the valley beyond the ridge. He and his men watched as officers with *samurai* swords at their sides walked around the command post and moved in and out of caves. One American sniper set to work, and in the next few hours shot twenty Japanese around that command post.

But the marines could not get off the hill and could not capture it. They sent bazookas and demolitions men and riflemen, and still the Japanese held out. The basic reason was their murderous fields of fire.

At the end of the day, the problem was how to get back down off the hill with the wounded. A smoke screen was set up by the artillery, and under its cover the men began to make their way off the hilltop. Not all of them could be reached, and had to be left up there as night was falling.

Those who were left on the hill waited for night and the coming of the Japanese. Two marines were lying a few feet apart when they heard a Japanese patrol coming. They put their ponchos over their heads and pretended to be dead. A Japanese soldier lifted the poncho of one, and the marine gave a start, whereupon he was killed. The other marine lay perfectly still practicing breath control, and when his poncho was lifted he did not stir. The Japanese then searched the "body." Finding nothing of military value, they put everything back in the pockets and went away.

That was the first patrol. Three more patrols came by and investigated this marine. One Japanese stuck a knife in his leg, and he did not stir. One felt his side, but felt the right side instead of the left, and the marine's wildly beating heart was not discovered. Next morning the marine was rescued from the hilltop.

The only real value of this failed effort to take Hill 382 was what the Americans learned about the defenses. The defense

124 IWO JIMA

of the hill, the Turkey Knob, the Amphitheater, and Minami village were all coordinated, and they all worked together almost perfectly. The blockhouse on Turkey Knob, the marines figured, was the center of communications and observation, and its walls were so thick that it seemed impervious to naval shells and artillery.

The Eighth Marines assaulted Hill Peter for the second day. They were supposed to have air support, but the bombers and fighters from the carriers were dropping so far ahead of the marines that the support did no good. The First Battalion did manage to get a flamethrower tank around the hill, and it assaulted the Japanese positions. The Ninth Marines fought all day around this hill, but at the end of five hours they still had not made any gains. The Japanese were extremely stubborn. They would come out, get shot, fall down, and then begin to throw grenades. If they were not killed outright they managed to crawl or stagger to an aid station and get their wounds treated and come out to fight again. But so it was, too, with the marines. Time and again, a marine would be sent down to the beach by medical officers, and would get down there, become lonely for his outfit, and turn around and come back to fight.

But this day, Captain Awatsu's 309th Independent Infantry Battalion, having fought its way from the first day on the slopes of Mt. Suribachi, ceased to exist. The Twenty-third Marines drove the battalion over against the Twenty-fifth Marines, who finished it off.

That night, there was no mortar fire support from the sea for the marines. The great miscalculation as to how long it would take to reduce Iwo Jima had caused the planners to order the mortar craft sent back to Saipan to prepare for the invasion of Okinawa, and so they left before the job on Iwo Jima was done. But in a way they were replaced by the Army's 509th Anti-Aircraft Battalion, which landed that day and began sending 90mm shells into the Japanese-held rocks on the west coast.

That night the Japanese tried to recapture the water wells, sending about a hundred troops to do the job. The marines in the front line spotted them, and the guns of the destroyers and the artillery were turned on the area. The Japanese raiding party was deciminated, and the survivors escaped back up to their defenses. That was the last attempt to recapture the wells. From this point on, the Japanese would have to rely on rainwater cisterns and stored waters.

CHAPTER SIXTEEN

And in the Second Week . . .

The marine casualties continued. One marine was sent down to the beach from Hill Peter after having fought most of the second morning of the second week. He had a case of heat rash so serious it covered him from head to toe, and the doctors said he should be evacuated from the island. But down on the beach he got lonely for his outfit, and after a couple of hours of wandering around and not seeing anyone he knew, he headed back up the terraces, and found his squad, fighting for Hill Peter. Before the hour was out he was dead, victim of a sniper bullet that hit him squarely between the eyes.

By this time, the ground around Hill 382 was so badly chewed up that tanks were useless. And 37 and 75mm guns could not be moved. That meant that the flamethrower and the satchel charges were the primary instruments of destruction of the Japanese emplacements. But sniper fire continued to be a very serious problem until the end of this second day, when the sniper nests above the East Boat Basin were dispersed. For the first time, the beaches of this area of the Fourth Division were clear of enemy fire and the bigger landing craft could come in. The *Columbia Victory* arrived with artillery ammunition, and shore parties worked all night moving ammunition for the guns. It was badly needed; the Corps artillery fired nearly 6,000 rounds of ammunition on this one day.

And in the Second Week . . .   127

The Twenty-third Marines were heading for the east end of Airfield No. 2, and the radio station, which had been destroyed days ago by artillery fire, but the remains still lay on the slope near Hill 382. They found minefields on the taxiways, and many pillboxes. So by Tuesday, of the second week, the advance was still mole-slow, and forward progress was marked by individual acts of heroism such as that of Private Wilson D. Watson, who had mastered the art of fighting with a BAR. He had knocked out several pillboxes on Monday. On Tuesday morning, he ran to the top of a hill and, firing the BAR from the hip, held the crest single-handed for fifteen minutes, and killed some sixty Japanese before any of his platoon joined him.

Thus the Third Division advanced in the marine line. The Ninth Marines went after Hill Oboe and Hill Peter.

At noon, the artillery put down a barrage of ten minutes. After that, the Ninth Marines began to move quickly. The First Battalion took Hill Peter, and then Hill Oboe, and the Second Battalion on the left kept going for 1,500 yards. This put them on the plateau, which was relatively level, and gave them Airfield No. 2.

But on the right of the Third Marine Division, the Fourth Division had the same sort of day that they had seen so often on Iwo Jima. After a barrage, five battalions started abreast in the line. The Twenty-third Marines were up against Hill 382 again.

The Japanese had improved their defenses with artillery on the crest, and those guns drove the tanks down the hill every time they tried to come up. The infantry managed to grab a clawhold on the northwest slope, but the top of the hill was still held by the Japanese by the end of the day. The fighting went into the night time, and still the Japanese did not give up the hilltop.

The Twenty-fourth Marines moved around south of Turkey Knob and the Amphitheater, but they made only about 200 yards along the east coast, and nearly nothing at the two strong points. The Twenty-third Marines fought hard all day and made no ground at all.

They inched forward and were thrown back, and at nighttime they were back to their line of departure of the morning. The day had meant nearly 800 casualties for the Fourth Division alone.

General Senda's Second Mixed Brigade was holding its line very well, although it too was taking heavy casualties. The Japanese were still getting some help from outside, although the *kamikazes*, by and large, had been a failure. From the other Bonin Island bases, planes had been dropping supplies by night, and this night they brought medical supplies and ammunition to the troops in this central island redoubt. The marines saw flares, and then after midnight they saw the parachutes falling.

In the area of the Twenty-fifth Marines the Fifth Reconnaissance Company had spent the last week hunting out snipers and clearing the captured areas, and had killed more than five hundred Japanese and captured a small number.

A few Japanese were beginning to surrender, although they had to be very careful as to how they did it, lest they be shot down or blown up by their fellows for violating the Japanese army's code of battle to the death. Wounded men, isolated from their fellows, had been surrendering. One Japanese medic was found asleep, or pretending to be asleep, in the Hill 382 area near the entrance to a cave. Marines who came up poked him with a bayonet. He had in his hand a stick with a white sock on it, and he readily marched to the rear and readily answered questions posed by the intelligence officers, and agreed to work with the psychological warfare team to persuade other Japanese to give up. He was, he said, Private Kunimatsu Kato, and he came from Fukushima Province in northern Honshu.

From information they gathered from Private Kato and others, the intelligence officers learned that the Japanese garrison on Iwo Jima was much stronger than they had estimated earlier. They had put the figure at 14,000. Now they revised it to 20,000. They were still considerably short of the mark, but they were getting closer.

On the west coast of Iwo Jima, the Twenty-seventh Marines relieved the Twenty-sixth Marines and went up against Hill 362 A after a heavy bombardment that involved destroyers offshore, corps artillery, and the divisional guns. Carrier planes also came in to strike the hill. The advance then began and made some progress, about 500 yards. They still had not reached the hill.

The ninth day on Iwo Jima, then, ended with some major changes, although the marines' battle still raged. A navy evacuation hospital was set up on the beach and began working that night. The Third, Fourth, and Fifth Divisional hospitals were all in operation. And that day the army Thirty-eighth Field Hospital began landing. A few army troops were on the island with special equipment, and the Air Force was preparing to move in and establish its fighter operations. Major General James Chaney, who would head the army garrison force, arrived with his staff and part of the 147th Army Infantry Regiment and the Seventh Fighter Command. Little liaison spotter planes arrived on the island in some strength, and after the eighth day they began to fly missions low over the Japanese lines, looking for the elusive targets that had evaded the naval spotters and the big ships.

The marines now had captured a third of the island, and moved to the west side as well as the east side. They were setting up showers utilizing the island hot springs. The Seabees had built roads and beach exits on the west side of the island, but they could not be used yet. The Japanese artillery in the north still commanded these beaches.

The first post office was established on the island in the Fourth Division area. And it was announced that the first plane would leave for Saipan bearing V-mail that night of the eighth day. The postmaster was prepared to handle 100,000 letters a day for the three divisions.

The PBM flying boats came to Iwo Jima and took over the job of flying search missions. Planes from the escort carrier *Anzio* sank a submarine to the west of Chichi Jima and then the I-368, an I-boat carrying *kaiten*, or suicide submarines. A destroyer sank another I-boat carrying suicide submarines.

Interviewed by correspondents, General Smith optimistically suggested that the Japanese were running out of steam. He said he expected that the island would fall in a few more days. This although the marines still had less than half of the island by February 28. But General Smith based his statement on intelligence that indicated the Japanese were running short of water and medical supplies. It might be expected, following the pattern of the past, they would stage one great suicide raid as they had on Saipan, and throw themselves by the hundreds into the American guns just to get it over with.

On Wednesday, February 28, the Third Marine Division made good gains down the center of the island. The Twenty-first Marines, relieved the battered Ninth Marines at dawn, and by 9 A.M. they were starting forward. Now they had a surprise and Colonel Nishi, the tank commander, had his little moment of glory. General Kuribayashi had ordered that the tanks be dug in, and they had been. But now the marines had come to the point that if the tanks did not move, they would be bypassed and destroyed without ever having had a chance to fight. So Colonel Nishi had permission at last to make a tank attack.

First came a barrage from the artillery for the Twenty-first Marines, and then the infantry began to move. The tanks had been freed that night before, and they came out this morning, throwing off their camouflage and mounds of dirt and beginning to advance. For a moment it seemed that they would rout the marines, but then Captain Edward Stephenson of Company I led his men forward in a combined attack with flamethrowers and bazookas, and in a matter of an hour had destroyed three tanks. Two more were hit by 20mm fire from strafing aircraft and knocked out. This left Colonel Nishi only three tanks. The Twenty-first Marine advance crashed through what was left of Motoyama village and stopped there at noon. They had gained 400 yards.

In the afternoon they advanced beyond the village, and at the end of the day controlled the high ground and had broken the center of the enemy line. Off to the northeast, they could see the landing strips of the unfinished No. 3 Airfield.

The Fourth Division continued to attack Hill 382 and virtually surrounded it this day. Company A of the Twenty-third Marines reached the back slope in early afternoon.

The whole attack was supported by the rocket trucks, which came up, fired their rockets, and retreated to reload time and again. The heavy artillery trained on the hill, and the bazookamen came up and fired missile after missile.

And in the Second Week . . . 131

The Twenty-fifth Marines continued to attack Turkey Knob and the Amphitheater. They brought up a 75mm pack howitzer which they had to take apart, and put in an amphtrac. Then they brought it to the scene, put it together, and fired eighty-five rounds into the Japanese fortification. But the Japanese held fast. Troops of the First Battalion almost encircled the knob, but then the Japanese on the top hurled down so many grenades that they had to fall back. So the end of the day came, and the Japanese still held the knob and the Amphitheater. As the Fourth Division leaders counted casualties that night, they saw that the division had suffered more than 4,000 killed and wounded in seven days of fighting.

That night of February 28, General Erskine called for his reserve regiment, the Third Marines, who were waiting in transports off Iwo Jima. Total marine casualties had passed the 8,000 mark. But General Holland Smith refused the request for the reserves. He still wanted to keep a fresh regiment for the Okinawa attacks.

The Twenty-seventh Marines of the Fifth Division moved forward toward Hill 362, and by noon the Third Battalion reached the foot of the hill. But during the assault on the hill itself grenades were flying back and forth like snowballs in a snowfight.

One marine threw back eight Japanese grenades that fell in his shell hole, until he ran out of luck and was killed trying to throw back the ninth one. The Japanese here were now freed from the restraint against attack, and later that afternoon, on the right of the hill a group of about 199 Japanese attacked down the hill trying to throw the marines off. The combat was hand-to-hand, and the Japanese were dispersed, but the marines did not capture the hill, and had to dig in that night on the slopes.

March 1 was notable as the day that the medical facilities of Iwo Jima became self-sustaining. With the three divisional hospitals operating and both a navy and army hospital ashore, there were enough beds and facilities to release the LST hospital ships, and they sailed for Saipan. In ten days, they had cared for more than 6,000 wounded men.

132 IWO JIMA

The southern half of Iwo Jima now began to have something of the air of a garrison area. New concerns had to be attended to, such as spraying the area with DDT to kill flies and suppress the spread of disease. Troop carrier planes and navy planes from the Marianas flew over, dropping medical supplies and repair parts.

That night, the Japanese made a new effort to capture water wells, sending in special forces equipped with bazookas and mortars. But the marines did not yield and the Japanese got no water, nor did any of the men of this mission get back to their own lines.

Admiral Soemu Toyoda, commander of the Japanese Combined Fleet, sent a message of encouragement to Admiral Ichimaru, blessing the Japanese for their efforts and asking them to fight on, as every minute of delay of the expected invasion of Japan itself was important to the home forces that were furiously trying to improve their defense capability. But within the message was the voice of doom, because Toyoda apologized for not being able to send any assistance to Ichimaru except submarines, and as far as the Japanese on Iwo Jima were concerned, the submarines were of no assistance at all. As they came into the Bonins, they were hunted down by the air forces and the destroyers and escorts.

March 1 opened with Japanese shelling by artillery that had been moved around in the caves and tunnels to new positions in the northern defense area. They shelled the west coast of Iwo Jima, alongside Airfield No. 1. This was the area that the Seabees had recently been building up as a supply area, and it was full of supply dumps, motor pools, and artillery.

Shortly after two o'clock in the morning, a Japanese shell hit in the Fifth Division's main ammunition dump, and in a minute the place was a roaring inferno of ammunition explosion, with everything from rifle ammunition to heavy artillery shells going off in all directions. The confusion in the area was almost total. Someone tripped the air raid alarm and it went off, so the men started searching the skies for planes that never arrived. Someone else tripped the gas alarm, mistaking exploding white phosphorous projectiles in the exploding dump for gas shells

And in the Second Week... 133

so there was a gas panic that lasted about ten minutes.

After the first shocking minutes, troops rallied and rushed into the dump to carry out shells. The excitement continued until after five o'clock in the morning, and many men were burned or injured in the process of saving the dump. One 105mm shell smashed into the corps artillery fire direction center and knocked out the communications of the artillery. The corps dump of telephone equipment was also set ablaze, and most of the telephone wire ashore was destroyed.

The engineers saved the dump, bringing up bulldozers that pushed sand over it, and by seven o'clock in the morning the fires were out and life was getting back to normal. The Fifth Marine Division had lost a quarter of its ammunition supply, but there had been no men killed.

That morning there was indeed an air raid, although it did not affect the men on the island. A Japanese torpedo plane came in and dropped a torpedo destined for the destroyer *Terry*, which missed. But that afternoon the *Terry* came in too close to shore and was hit by coastal guns of the Japanese defense. Eleven men were killed and nineteen were wounded, and the *Terry* soon started for Pearl Harbor, limping along with only one engine in commission.

That day the Fifth Marine Division had the show. The Twenty-eighth Marines went back into action after a rest from their efforts in taking Suribachi. Their assignment was Hill 362 A. And they swept to the top in an early morning charge, but when they got there they found an 80-foot cliff dropping off into a ravine behind the hill. On both sides the Japanese had constructed cunning defenses, utilizing the natural caves and digging more defenses. An antitank ditch ran across the bottom of the ravine in the middle; the only way into the area was around the edges.

Company A started around to the right and Company B on the left. Captain Aaron G. Wilkins of Company A called for volunteers, and one who volunteered was Corporal Tony Stein, who had the stinger, and who had medals from Guadalcanal and a citation for a Medal of Honor from D Day in Iwo Jima. Corporal Stein and his stinger volunteered for a patrol to clear the ridge of snipers. The patrol consisted of twenty-nine men. But only seven came back, and Tony Stein and the stinger were not among them. Captain Wilkins was also killed. He was the last of the original company commanders in the battalion.

The going was as difficult as ever. Sergeant Al Eutsey was crawling forward on the right of Hill 362 A when he was hit by shrapnel.

"A grenade or mortar landed at my left side, a fragment cutting the thick strap of my pack and entering my left chest. My head was ringing, my side felt numb, and I was bleeding. In a few moments Corpsman Keith Hawkins was on the spot giving me first aid. Mortars and grenades were pounding the area as he stuffed the hole in my chest with gauze. A team of stretcher bearers reached me, loaded me up and started back. By now the Japs had opened up on the stretcher bearers. The first thing I knew, I had been dropped in a ditch as the team ran for cover. I believe one of the men was killed or wounded. Ended up with a different set of bearers, and I got dumped a couple of more times due to enemy fire before they got me back to an ambulance jeep. It had stretcher racks, and I was put on facing the rear. The jeep was drawing fire and took off in a hurry. I lay and watched the shells bursting behind us as we moved. Our luck held out and we got back okay."

Company B started around the other shoulder of Hill 362 A. Captain Robert Wilson, the commander, was wounded and for the second time since the fighting began, First Lieutenant Charles Weaver took over the company. The first time had been on D Day after Captain Dwayne Mears had been killed assaulting pillboxes with a .45 caliber pistol.

The attack went well, and near the shore the Third Battalion made progress. But at the end of the day only the crest of Hill 362 A was in marine hands. And the day had cost the Fifth Marine Division six more officers killed.

In the center of the line, the Third Division moved forward from Motoyama village, turning to the east as they reached the wider part of the island. But the gain for the day was 500 yards maximum.

The Fourth Division assault was concentrated against Hil

382 and Turkey Knob. At one point, the men of the Second Battalion of the Twenty-fourth Marines got to the top, but the defenders would not give up. By nightfall the hill and Turkey Knob were still in Japanese hands. By day's end the Fourth Division's casualties had risen to 5,600 officers and men. That night they shared the hill with the Japanese, who were more than usually active in their infiltration.

That day, more Japanese surrendered, which was a sign that the battle was coming to an end. The marines noticed that artillery fire was not as intense and that it did not last as long. Nor did the Japanese seem to be firing as much with their automatic weapons. All this indicated the enemy might be growing short of ammunition.

On the next day, March 2, which was D + 11, the Fourth Division overran all of Hill 382 and took the line forward 150 yards beyond the hill. The unit involved, the Second Battalion of the Twenty-fourth Marines, paid heavily for the success. Company E alone lost five officers that day, two of them killed. Company F nearly lost its commanding officer, Captain Walter Ridlon. During the fighting he climbed up on top of a knoll behind the front line and sat down to direct operations. Suddenly the knoll shook and the captain was tumbled off. In a bunker beneath the hill a Japanese 75mm gun had looped fire on targets on the east beach. The captain and two other marines found an opening in the bunker and put a satchel charge in it. Afterwards they blew the rest of the bunker apart with grenades.

That day Hill 382 was won, but no one was celebrating. Turkey Knob, the Amphitheater, and Minami village were holding out just as firmly as ever, and much marine blood was spilled around these places, without any significant gains. At Turkey Knob the marines sent eight tanks against the big blockhouse there. Some of the tanks were equipped with 75mm guns, and some with flamethrowers. They shot off scores of 75mm shells and a thousand gallons of flamethrower fuel. As long as they were attacking, the blockhouse was silent. But when the assault ended, the blockhouse came back to life. The Japanese had simply retired to their caves far below the surface at the height of the attack, and when it ended they came up again.

136 IWO JIMA

The day ended with the Meatgrinder still in operation, although one fourth of it had been knocked out at Hill 382. But even there, the hill would come to life now and again. The Japanese were obviously moving around in the tunnels underneath that connected all these positions. Marine spotter planes were busy all around that area all day, and one plane had a particular mission, to take photographs of the Meatgrinder positions. The ground had been so torn up in the past few days that the maps of the marine commanders no longer meant anything, and new ones would have to be drawn during the night from aerial photographs.

The Third Division spent the day working in the island center section, advancing 1,500 yards toward Hill 362 B. On the right, the division was only about 1,500 yards from the coast, but up against a sector called Cushman's Pocket, which was full of Japanese.

Here Lieutenant Colonel Nishi had his headquarters in a cave complex that occupied three levels underground. A curving passage led to the top, and it was hung with about 50 blankets, which were supposed to absorb the heat from flamethrowers. Here Nishi and his men were holding out, obeying orders and not risking any more confrontation with the enemy than necessary, but continuing to fight.

There were "rear areas" now—not really rear areas, because there was still no place on Iwo Jima that the Japanese could not reach with their shelling except the far side of Mt. Suribachi—but rear areas where the marines had a chance to take it a little bit easier and to relax.

A road had been built up the slopes of Mt. Suribachi and about fifty yards from the beach line the marines had erected a sign:

SURIBACHI HEIGHTS REALTY COMPANY
Ocean View
Cool Breezes
Free Fireworks, Nightly!

Another marine who had improved his foxhole put up a sign outside:

NOTICE
This Foxhole Is Privately Owned
And Was Not Constructed With the Help Of
The Federal Housing Administration

On top of a 30-foot cliff north of the No. 1 Airfield, a group of marine correspondents and photographers had taken over a blockhouse that had been a Japanese communications center. After they found these luxurious quarters they moved in. Every morning they would go out on their assignments and in the evening they would return to the blockhouse to write their stories, clean up their camera equipment and sleep in relative comfort. In the morning when they left they would hang out a sign in 6-inch letters:

DANGEROUS!!!
MINED AND BOOBYTRAPPED!!

This ploy worked for two days, but then the demolition engineers came by, took the warning at face value, and blew the blockhouse into a thousand pieces. For the rest of the campaign the marine correspondents lived in foxholes.

On Suribachi, where it was realized now that the fighting was ended and the stink of the dead bodies had subsided, one Fifth Division marine had put up a sign at the entrance to the cave he had taken over:

ICHIMOTO'S INN
Under New Management
Soon Available to Personnel
Of the U.S. Army

And so on the night of March 1, darkness came down again on the marines, in the front it was as tense and awful as it had been for nearly two weeks, but behind the lines, the marines were able to joke and reminisce already about the campaign that had not yet ended.

"My God! There's Smitty! Hey, Smitty, I heard you was dead. Damn you! I was feeling sorry for you!"

One marine grinned, "I had some coffee today. Felt like a million bucks!"

An officer confided, "All the officers I came overseas with are gone now—all killed or wounded."

"Hey, what day is it? When's Sunday? I want to go to church on Sunday."

"Where's the guy who said we'd take this island in five days? I hope he's up in the line right now . . ."

But that line wasn't very far away. It grew darker, and a mortar shell burst nearby.

"I'm gettin' out of here. You guys can stay here and get picked off if you wanna. Me, I'm going back to the CP."

Another marine spoke up: "There's two kinds of marines on this island—the lucky and the unlucky. Let's hit the sack. It's seven o'clock."

And at the command posts, and wherever else there were powerful radio receivers, the sounds of American dance bands drifted forth, or the wise words of Tokyo Rose, and Radio Tokyo's reports of how General Kuribayashi and his men were annihilating the U.S. Marines.

CHAPTER SEVENTEEN

The Meatgrinder

In principle, General Kuribayashi was quite right in his approach to the defense of Iwo Jima. He had intended to make it so costly in terms of killed and wounded Americans that the authorities would take a second look at their whole program of offense against Japan. The plan nearly worked. By the middle of the second week several storms had blown over Iwo Jima.

From the outset the heavy marine casualties had shocked the military leaders and the public. The war correspondents wrote about the carnage on the beaches. In the first twelve days of the Iwo Jima invasion, more than a million words of newspaper stories were radioed from the command ship *Eldorado* to American publications. Most of those words tended to emphasize the difficulties and the casualties. At home the American people reacted with shock, and some, like the Hearst newspaper chain, were extremely critical of the American leadership in the Pacific. The twenty-two Hearst newspapers, the *Chicago Tribune*, the *New York Daily News* and the *Washington Times Herald* led a campaign to transfer leadership in the Pacific from Admiral Nimitz to General MacArthur.

The editorial campaign was an attempt to undermine the American leadership, but it failed. It did arouse enormous public concern. One woman wrote Secretary of the Navy James Forrestal, "Please, for God's sake, stop sending our finest youth to be murdered on places like Iwo Jima."

Forrestal replied to this letter publicly.

140 IWO JIMA

"On December 7, 1941, the Axis confronted us with a simple choice: fight or be overrrun. There was then, and is now, no other possibility. Having chosen to fight, we had then, and we have now no final means of winning battles except through the valor of the marine or army soldier, who, with rifle and grenade, storms enemy positions, takes them, and holds them. There is no shortcut or easy way." And the fierce fighting went on.

By the middle of the second week, Iwo Jima had become sidebar copy, and most of the stories about it were relegated to the inside pages of the newspapers. The Allies were driving deep into Germany, and Allied leaders in Europe were speculating on the day that the Nazi empire would collapse completely. The reporters began to leave the island, heading for Guam and the invasion of Okinawa that would come in a few weeks. About twenty civilian reporters were left on Iwo Jima. The rest were marine combat correspondents, and the stories that they wrote were delayed by red tape and censorship. Indeed, censorship had come into play recently for the first time in World War II. The mechanics of censorship had always existed, but in the past only General MacArthur had invoked tight censorship, and most of that activity was to make sure that MacArthur received a good press. The navy at Pearl Harbor had relentlessly told the truth, even when it hurt, such as in the grinding naval campaign at Guadalcanal, where the Japanese seemed to win all the battles until the end. But now, in the concern lest the enemy be encouraged by the high casualties it was inflicting at Iwo Jima and by the use of the *kamikaze* suicide divers on the fleet, Admiral Nimitz used censorship to conceal the true facts.

By the second week of the battle, conditions ashore had continued steadily to improve. Mess halls were set up ashore for the Seabees and service troops and they began to get at least one hot meal a day. The marines in the line were not that lucky, but a beached LST was converted into a mess hall and began to serve hot meals to marines.

On the last day of February, the Third Division had orders from General Schmidt to take the rest of the high ground on their front and then to drive to the northern shore line. It sounded easy, since the last resistance around the No. 2 Airfield had been knocked out. The Twenty-first Marines were given the job. They moved forward that first morning, until the advance was stalled just before noon. It took another barrage in midday to get the offensive going again. The marines then moved into and through Motoyama village, the great settlement on Iwo Jima in days gone by but now a pile of rubble, with Japanese snipers and machine guns in almost every cranny. The Twenty-first Marines managed to take the high ground and broke through the Japanese main line. By nightfall of that day they had seized the ground overlooking the unfinished No. 3 Airfield. But they were still a long way from Iwo Jima's north shore.

Since almost the beginning, the Fourth Division had been up against the Meatgrinder, and it still was. The intricate defense system involved the Amphitheater, Turkey Knob, Minami village, and Hill 382. The Hill sometimes seemed about to fall apart, but it was all illusory. The Japanese might lose the ground on top, but as night came they moved around in their tunnels and came out to fight again, day after day. The major assault on the Meatgrinder had begun on D + 6, February 24. Then General Clifton B. Cates had told the Twenty-fourth and Twenty-fifth Marines to try to find a weak spot in the Japanese front, and keep on slugging until they did. So four assault battalions, nearly 4,000 marines in all, had moved against this maze of fortifications.

The attack had been begun that day by the Third Battalion of the Twenty-third Marines, who had been preceded into action by a thorough bombardment. The Japanese were silent during the bombardment, but the minute that the marines began to move they had been hit with extremely heavy fire. Six tanks had come up and four of them had been knocked out in the first minutes. The two survivors tried to go ahead but were mired in the volcanic ash, sinking their treads. That first day, in what was one long series of acts of bravery, members of one platoon of the marines clawed their way without flamethrowers or tanks to the summit of Hill 382, but there they were cut off by counter-attack, and it took two hours for them to pull back under a smokescreen. That was the night that a dozen wounded men had been left on the hill until after dark. At the end of that first day, a nose count showed that nearly five hundred men had been lost to gain a hundred yards.

It was apparent at the end of that first day that something had to be done to soften up the Japanese in this complex, but what? The first attempt was to do the softening by extremely heavy shelling, and it began on that same afternoon of February 24, at about 4:30. Then for fifteen minutes the carrier aircraft tried to do the job. The assault did just what it was supposed to do. It drove the Japanese off the hill, but instead of running away, they simply retreated to their caves in the mountain, thirty and forty feet down, and waited. The real accomplishment of the barrage that afternoon was to make it possible for the marines to collect their dead and wounded from the hill that night. But that night, the Japanese were up out of their caves, and trying to infiltrate the marine lines. Shortly before midnight, thirty Japanese, many of them officers and noncoms wielding sabers, hit the company of Captain Donald Callahan. "Some of them spoke English," he said. "They jumped into foxholes and yelled like marines. But their English was pretty phoney and we spotted them."

The marines raced. Next morning, twenty Japanese bodies were found around the foxholes. No marines were lost that night.

Marine Correspondent Jim Lucas reported on this stage of the battle. "This bastardly battle just goes on and on from one ridge to another. When will it end? And will anybody be alive when it does?"

On February 25, General Cates was urging that Hill 382 be taken before nightfall. The First and Second Battalions of the Twenty-third Marines made the first assault that day, and found the Meatgrinder intact and spitting fire as fast as ever. The first sign of the marine movement brought hails of fire from Hill 382 and the Turkey Knob. Company C of the First Battalion was ambushed by crossfire, and within half an hour seventeen men were killed and twenty-six others wounded. They did, however, get to the base of Hill 382, largely through the efforts of Private First Class Douglas Jacobson. He was a rifleman, but when the going got tough and the bazookaman next to him was cut down, he snatched up the weapon and a satchel of rockets and explosives. For the next half hour, he fought his own private war against the Japanese. He sprinted up to one pillbox that was spitting fire and blasted it with the bazooka. The pillbox machine gun stopped chattering. He vaulted over a boulder and found another emplacement. He blasted it with the bazooka too. Then he took on a concrete blockhouse, and another, and another, and a fourth, until he ran out of ammunition. He had to quit then. When he came back to the line, somebody asked him how he had managed to handle the bazooka by himself. The book said it was a two-man weapon.

Company I made it to the top of Hill 382 that day, but it was the same old story. They could not hold up there; the Japanese fire was too heavy and too concentrated. As one of the marines of the company said:

"Our tanks couldn't operate on the rocky hillside. It was impossible to bring up flamethrowers and demolitions experts. Our men had to fight their way through terrain flanked by enemy guns. Bazookas proved to be the invaluable weapon, firing point-blank into enemy positions."

But after four and a half hours of fighting to get up, Company I had to go back down and pull away from this hill once again.

At 4:30 that afternoon, General Cates called a halt again to the day's attacks. It was raining hard and would continued to rain until 9:30. The marines had gained another two hundred yards, but they had lost another five hundred men. That night, marines heard the movement of the Japanese as they reinforced Turkey Knob and Hill 382. And that night, General Kuribayashi told Tokyo that he could still hold Iwo Jima, if the navy would strike the Americans with battleships, submarines, and the air force. But there was no response to his request. Except for submarines and suicide air missions, the navy had nothing left with which to strike the enemy, and their operations had been so delayed that the *kamikaze* corps in the homeland was not yet organized to act.

Hill 382 was not just a hill, the marines had now discovered. It was a complex, and it had to be subdued before the advance could really continue. The First and Third Battalions of the

144 IWO JIMA

Twenty-third Marines now took charge of the attack here. Again in the morning there was the bombardment, and again the marines began their push at its end. But the enemy fire was as fierce as ever.

The Twenty-fifth Marines attacked Turkey Knob, and fought all day again. The Sherman tanks came up and were hit by 47mm Japanese antitank guns. Two tanks were knocked out in short order. Another was hit, but managed to limp away and hide under a ridge. Six rocket launcher trucks came up and sent 431 rounds of 4.5-inch rockets into the western slope and summit of Hill 382. Did it do any good? The marines liked to think so, but on the line it seemed that all the rocketing did was make the Japanese as angry as a nest of hornets. The Third Battalion of the Twenty-third Marines moved up the hill time and again only to be thrown back. Part of one platoon finally made the crest. In the ruins of the wrecked radar tower they held for two and a half hours, until they ran out of ammunition and had to go back down the hill they had climbed so many times before. The First Battalion tried to drive around the base of Hill 382 and ran into the same sort of fields of fire and heavy resistance. But by inching forward, sometimes one man at a time, the battalion managed to put a line around the hill by midafternoon.

So that day the Twenty-third Marines were hitting Hill 382, and the Twenty-fifth Marines were hitting Turkey Knob. By midafternoon the First Battalion had moved to a line about halfway around the base of Turkey Knob. The Second Battalion tried to link up with the Third around the northwest side of the Knob but had no success. After five hours, the battalion had gained a hundred yards, and then had to retreat to the original line of departure.

The Third Battalion had almost the same experience. The Japanese simply overpowered the attackers with firepower and did not allow them to pass.

That afternoon General Cates was annoyed with Colonel John Lanigan, commander of the Twenty-fifth Marines, because he could not get in touch with him all afternoon. Lanigan had been up front trying to find that soft spot that General Cates wanted.

So the ninth day on Iwo Jima ended with the assault apparently no nearer success. General Kuribayashi would have been gratified to hear that the Marines had found no weak spot, but they knew that eventually they must find one. What they had to do was dig in for another night, and on the next day start a new attack and hope for the moment of breakthrough.

On the tenth day, 6,000 marines began another assault against the Meatgrinder. It started as usual with an air bombardment and naval assault, and then with the marines trying to advance. But the fire from the Knob, Hill 382, the Amphitheater, and Minami was as devastating as ever.

By late afternoon, Hill 382 and Turkey Knob were surrounded, but their slopes and tops were still held by the Japanese.

It was now obvious that there was no weak point in the defense and that only slogging could do the job. This meant blood. Colonel Lanigan's Twenty-fifth Marines came back in a fresh attempt to take the Meatgrinder. Several times that day the troops were faced by crisis from heavy mortar fire and grenades. Tanks were of little help, because they could not move in the terrain. At 4:45, General Cates ordered the lines consolidated. This took another two hours and once again needed the help of a smoke screen laid down by mortars to be effective. It looked hopeless.

But that night, in a battle summary, Colonel Edwin Pollock, the division intelligence officer, told the general that he was sure General Kuribayashi's communications were falling apart, and that the Japanese would not be able to mount a counteroffensive against the marines. (The fact was that Kuribayashi had no intention of mounting a counterattack against the marines. His whole policy was attrition.) He also said that the division had cracked the central defense core of Hill 382 and Turkey Knob. The end was now in sight. But they had to be careful because the attempts at infiltration would now grow stronger.

Pleasant words for the general. But what did they mean in terms of the marines who did the fighting and the dying?

It was simply speculation.

Twice that night, bands of Japanese marauders sneaked down the ravines and tried to get at the marines. But they were exposed by parachuted flares, and almost to a man these two attempts were wiped out. On March 1, the Fifth Marine Division managed to surround the base of Hill 362 A and to get up on the crest as well. But across the island the Twenty-fourth Regiment made another attempt to take Hill 382, only to come under a sustained Japanese artillery bombardment that lasted three hours. After that, the marines tried again to advance and were assailed by heavy automatic fire from Turkey Knob. By midafternoon, they had gained only 150 yards, and one company was pinned down on the slope of Hill 382. Late in the afternoon, marines of the Second Battalion got to the top of the hill and started to dig in along the western edge. A hundred yards to the east, the Japanese manned a strong complex of reinforced positions that spouted machine gun fire and mortar fire. Hand-to-hand combat resulted, and the two sides battled on the top of the hill until sunset. It was a standoff. But the marines held a part of the top of Hill 382. Could they hold it as night was falling? Company E was left up there to try, and they did hold that night. General Cates had the feeling that General Kuribayashi's defenses were almost ready to crack. But they had not cracked yet.

On March 2, the Meatgrinder was still in operation. The intricate system of Japanese tunnels and caves still made it possible for the Japanese to come back again after a position had been "won" by the marines. It was a lesson in strategy that the marines were learning the hard way. All these days of bombardment, all the explosives that could be hurled at the island had been hurled, and still the Japanese positions were almost impregnable. The Japanese real losses came from problems with water and provisions and medical supplies. Had they been supplied during the campaign, it is quite possible that the Japanese defense plan would have paid off. It was very close to doing so on Iwo Jima, with a loss of American public support for the war that was equalled only with the greatest of difficulty by the civilian leaders of the American military.

On the morning of March 2, General Cates ordered the attack to begin with a probe ninety minutes before the main assault. Se the marines of the First Battalion of the Twenty-fifth Marines jumped off at 6:30 in the morning to envelop Turkey Knob. But the 900 men of the battalion moved into an ambush. They were fighting in an area of about three city blocks, and the Japanese had many positions on the slopes from which they put out a withering crossfire against the marines. Cover was scarce in the ravine in front of the knob and scarcer on the slopes. At the top was the blockhouse of the Japanese, which had so far resisted air and artillery fire for many days. Now the marines were too close to the enemy for air support and artillery fire.

It was afternoon before the tanks began to come up. Eight Sherman tanks roared up through the volcanic ash, taking fire from mortars and Japanese antitank guns. But they did not get far, until the marines brought up armored bulldozers and carved paths through the rubble. Then two flamethrowers came up and poured more flame, and the tanks fired more 75mm shells into the blockhouse and the other defenses.

By later afternoon, the patrols of the marines were less than fifty yards from the Japanese defenses. The Japanese artillery and machine gun fire made the difference, and at 4:30 in the afternoon the word came from above to call off the attack. Turkey Knob was still holding out.

The Twenty-fifth had spent the day battering at Turkey Knob, while the Twenty-fourth Marines ran a three-battalion attack to drive the Japanese from the top of their half of Hill 382. The western ridge was held by Company E, which was nearly exhausted and reduced to half strength in its night effort to hold the top of the ridge. Now the Japanese were counterattacking in the morning across the no-man's-land that separated the two ridges. The marines had to have help from the men down below. They called for the help, and Company F brought it, although at a heavy price in casualties as they came up the slope.

Company E lost its commanding officer, and then the next in line, Second Lieutenant Reich took over the company. He was the only officer left. The fight continued, a struggle to the death.

It was 3:30 in the afternoon when the men of Fox Company, or what was left of it, managed to get to the top of Hill 382 to join the men of Company E. So the American position on top of the hill was strengthened for this second night. The machine guns of both sides clattered all night long, and star shells illuminated the battlefield in brief stretches. The marines could hear the Japanese moving through the tunnels underground as they regrouped to strengthen the defenses for the next morning. General Kuribayashi had now moved his headquarters from its deep concrete blockhouse east of the No. 3 Airfield site to a cave near Kitano Point, where he would make his last stand. That night, the stretcher bearers carried the last of the Fourth Division's 610 casualties from the front down to the hospitals and to the cemetery on the side of Mt. Suribachi. But the Japanese still held out on Hill 382 and Turkey Knob.

CHAPTER EIGHTEEN

Attrition

At dawn on March 1, General Erskine had taken a landing craft out to the command ship *Auburn* to argue his case for the release of the Third Marine Regiment to his Third Division. He had been refused because Admiral Turner and General Smith had agreed that, with 50,000 marines on Iwo Jima, there was not room for any more. Their real reason was to save the regiment in order to have fresh troops for the assault on Japan.

Erskine did not look at it that way. He had been given the assignment of taking the north shore of the island, and he wanted those three thousand men of the Third Marines and attached units. The need was not desperate, but he wanted to keep his casualties down. The Third Division was expected to capture an area larger than those assigned to either the Fourth or the Fifth Marine divisions.

General Schmidt, the commander of the Fifth Amphibious Corps, agreed with General Erskine. But when Erskine got to the command ship he found "Howling Mad" Smith obdurate. The troops would not be released. The real villain was Admiral Turner, and that became clear as Smith walked General Erskine to the gangway and in parting said, "Fight the battle with the troops you have—at least for the time being," which was as close as he would come to admitting that he did not know how much more desperate the situation ashore was going to become.

General Erskine was back at his command post by seven o'clock that morning and had ordered the attack of the division to begin. Three regiments attacked without naval bombardment or air support and with only fifteen minutes of shelling from the artillery. The assault was begun by the Second and Third Battalions of the Twenty-first Marines and the Third Battalion of the Ninth Marines. Their objective was to push through Motoyama village and seize the uncompleted third airfield.

The marines were surprised to find that resistance was very light. They gained 500 yards by noon and controlled most of the airfield. The Japanese had moved back to a new line of defense.

At 12:30, Marine artillery began a barrage to open the way for more gains and tanks joined the attack. Another three hundred yards were gained in the afternoon, but by midafternoon the bypassed bunkers and concealed pillboxes created problems in the rear of the advance, so General Erskine called a halt at 4:30. The marines were now near the base of Hill 362 B and Hill 362 C.

The Twenty-eighth Marines of the Fifth Division had taken Hill 362 A on March 1, as noted, with the loss of Tony Stein and other heroes, and then faced Nishi Ridge. On the night of March 2, their front stretched a thousand yards in front of Nishi Ridge. But their casualties had been very high. On the night of March 2, the Fourth Division counted the casualties from the beginning. They came to 6,000.

On March 1, Lieutenant Colonel Chandler Johnson of the Twenty-eighth Marines Second Battalion had been blown to bits in the assault on Nishi Ridge, and the battalion had been taken over by the executive officer, Major Thomas Pearce.

The pressure went on. The Meatgrinder was not yet in American hands, nor had it fallen at the end of March 2. So much had been accomplished, but it seemed there was so much more to do. The Third Marine Division had captured Hill 357, and one of its officers predicted that there was nothing important now to stop their path to the sea. He was wrong. That night, the Japanese mounted an attack to retake the hill. They failed, but next morning 163 Japanese bodies on the slope attested to the courage of the attack.

And so came the morning of March 3, which for the Fifth Marine Division was a day of horror and of valor. It was the day of the battle for Nishi Ridge. It began in the hours of darkness, when Japanese infiltrators began moving among the boulders to attack. A firefight ranged all along the Fifth Division's line below Nishi Ridge. Sergeant William Harrell was on outpost duty ten yards in front of the American line with Private First Class Andrew Carter, who was on watch when he saw the first Japanese. He awakened Sergeant Harrell. Both men opened fire and killed several Japanese. Carter's rifle misfired and he cursed the sand and went back for another weapon. In the meantime, a grenade wobbled into their foxhole and exploded, Harrell found he could not move his left arm or leg and he was bleeding. He was trying to reload his carbine with one hand when two Japanese sprang from the ravine to the edge of the foxhole. One was swinging a *samurai* sword with two hands, and the other was throwing grenades. Carter tried to fire his weapon. It misfired. He grabbed up a Japanese rifle, a souvenir he had carried since D Day, and bayoneted the sword-wielding officer. But the sword sliced deep into his left hand.

Sergeant Harrell gave up trying to reload the carbine and picked up his .45 pistol. He killed the second Japanese. He thought he was dying, and so he sent Carter back to the command post. Carter left, promising to return.

Harrell lay in his hole hoping the Japanese would forget about him. But a Japanese soldier jumped into the hole and another crouched on the rim. The first Japanese slammed a grenade against his helmet to arm it, dropped the grenade, and leaped out of the hole. Harrell shot him with the .45, but the grenade was still there. He grabbed it and threw it to the edge of the hole, where it exploded, killing the second Japanese soldier, but also blowing off Harrell's right hand. More Japanese came. And Carter came back with litter bearers and they rescued Sergeant Harrell. Marines counted twelve Japanese bodies around Harrell's hole in the ground. For his action he received the Medal of Honor.

Hill 362 B still barred the advance of the Fifth Marine Division this day. They had replaced the Third Division on its slopes. The fighting was so heavy by midmorning of D + 12 that it seemed to be a day made for the corpsmen. One of them, Pharmacist's Mate Third Class Jack Williams, had treated fourteen marines since the jump off at 7:45. Just before noon, he found another wounded marine and was crouching in a shallow hole treating him when a sniper opened up on the hole. Williams was hit three times, in the belly, but he finished bandaging the other marine's wounds before he tried to halt the hemorrhage from his belly. And then he patched up another marine. Sniper fire was all around, but he knew he had to get back to the lines and bring help for the other two marines or they would die on the battlefield. He clasped his arms about his belly and moved forward. A shot rang out—a sniper had struck again—and Pharmacist's Mate Third Class Williams fell dead. When other corpsmen found the two marines later, they were still alive and they told the story. Williams received a posthumous Medal of Honor.

It was one of five won that day in the Fifth Division.

Besides Harrell's and Williams', Pharmacist's Mate Second Class George Wahlen earned another Medal of Honor. He should not even have been in action that day because he had already been wounded twice by mortar shells. Each time he had talked his way back into action after treatment at the division hospital. His argument was that there were only three medics left in his Second Battalion of the Twenty-sixth Marines. He was involved in the fight for Hill 362 B. The battalion moved 300 yards that day across flat terrain without too much trouble. But then they found themselves in the rugged arroyos and jutting rocks that had stopped the Twenty-eighth Marines. The combat there was hand-to-hand with flamethrowers, bazookas, and hand grenades against the enemy machine guns, *samurai* swords, rifles, and bayonets. Wahlen heard the cry "Corpsman! Corpsman! Over here!"

He headed toward the sound with his satchel of medications. A blast of small arms fire hit him from pointblank range. He collapsed in a pool of blood. But he survived, and lived for his Medal.

A few hundred yards away, Corporal William Caddy was sitting with two other marines in a shell hole at the base of the hill. Small arms fire was popping overhead and mortars and grenades were exploding all around. One of them arched into the shell hole. Caddy saw it in the air, and lunged on top of the grenade, taking the blast in his chest and stomach. That was the fourth Medal of Honor of the day for the division.

The fifth went to Corporal Charles J. Berry. Since 8:30 the First Battalion of the Twenty-eighth Marines had been fighting in the gorges north and west of Nishi Ridge. They had been promised air support, but the mission had been cancelled by rain and low ceiling. The ground was a sea of volcanic mud and the tanks could not function. The artillery spotters could not function because of poor visibility. Rifles plugged up with the muck.

In their protected positions, the Japanese were not subject to these problems, and they were cutting down marines right and left from their cover. By late afternoon, the battalion had advanced less than a hundred yards, and had more than a hundred casualties. Late afternoon became evening. The marines dug in as best they could and waited for the infiltration by the Japanese. Berry was one of three riflemen who dug a foxhole on top of the edge of a hill and settled in for the night. Two men would try to sleep while the third stood watch. Sleep was impossible in the racket of the machine guns and the artillery that continued far into the night, and they could see Japanese moving around from one position to another.

Just after two o'clock in the morning, one of the other marines nudged Berry. "Here come the Nips."

A fusillade of fire passed over their foxhole and a hail of grenades surrounded it. One rolled over the top into the hole. Berry covered it with his body and died in the grenade explosion. But the Japanese got harsh treatment from other marines; when morning came, ninety-seven bodies were counted in this area. The other two wounded marines were rescued and Berry's body was taken back. He had won the fifth Medal of Honor in the division that day.

That night, when General Rockey checked his maps, he saw that the Fifth Division had gained 150 yards in some places and 600 yards in other places. But how long could they keep

154 IWO JIMA

it up? The Twenty-sixth Marines had lost more than half the 3,300 officers and men who had landed on D Day.

Yet aboard the command ships, the picture looked slightly brighter. There was a distinct slowing in the fierceness of the Japanese attack against the Fifth Division, and the Third Marine Division had pierced the center of the Japanese line. Only in the area of the Fourth Division was the Meatgrinder still unconquered, and there the slaughter had continued all day on D + 12.

The assault on Hill 382 had begun at 6:30 in the morning by the Twenty-fourth Marines and against Turkey Knob by the Twenty-third Marines. The marines had moved without bombardment or air attack in an attempt to catch the Japanese off guard. Some men from F company of the Second Battalion of the Twenty-fourth reached the hill top and lay there. Then they moved, sealing off caves and pillboxes with demolitions and flamethrowers. Captain Walter Ridlon's men found themselves on a mound that turned out to be a 75mm gun bunker. The bunker began spouting cannon shells. Captain Ridlon's men stuffed the apertures with demolition charges and blew it up.

Such stories began to have a familiar ring to them, so often had they been repeated in the saga of the Meatgrinder. The trouble now, as before, was the heavy casualty rate caused by the nature of the Japanese defense, especially among junior officers and noncommissioned officers.

Company E was under the command of Lieutenant William Crecink that morning. He was wounded and evacuated before nine o'clock in the morning. Second Lieutenant Dick Reich then took over the company until a captain could arrive. The captain came up and was promptly wounded in the leg and carried back to the rear. Lieutenant Reich took command again. Captain Robert O'Mealia, a bandmaster, came up. He was killed by mortar fire in the first ten minutes after arrival. But by this time there was no need for Lieutenant Reich to take command again, because so many other men of the company had been killed and wounded that only a dozen were left. They were merged into Company F.

Turkey Knob, the Amphitheater, and Minami village defenses still erupted fire after a week of heavy attack by every conceivable weapon in the marine arsenal, from 16-inch naval guns, to satchel charges and flamethrowers. A four-room-blockhouse on Turkey Knob still spouted gunfire. Mines were strewn all around the building, so tank operation was impossible until the mines could be cleared by demolition teams. The level of fire from the blockhouse and surrounding defenses was so heavy at all times that the demolitions teams could not work to clear the mines.

In the Amphitheater, after a week of operations, another network of blockhouses, pillboxes, and spider traps had to be demolished, one at a time. Even after Minami village was reduced to rubble, it still contained sniper positions and mortar pits.

By noon of D + 12, the attack had settled down to another contest of sheer brutality. Demolitions teams and flamethrowers worked over the caves, the bypassed bunkers, and the bypassed pillboxes. Sherman tanks braved the mine-riddled paths to help. The marine artillery was trained on Japanese positions that were seldom more than a hundred yards ahead of the marine line. As had now become usual on Iwo Jima, progress meant individual effort by individual marines and fire teams and squads. That's how the offensive was pressed, and as it had been from the beginning, the cost in casualties was high. By the end of this day, the deepest penetration in the Amphitheater area was 300 yards. The blockhouse on top of Turkey Knob was still as strong as ever. The real progress was on Hill 382, where the marines of Captain Ridlon's Company F had pushed across from the western slope through the no-man's-land of the past three days, and moved down the eastern slope. General Cates predicted confidently that the marines would close down the Meatgrinder forever on the next day.

As dawn arrived on March 4, which was D Day + 13, clouds hung low above the island, and the rain was falling. The bad weather caused cancellation of the air strikes and the artillery spotting missions by the liaison planes. The marines were so close to the Japanese lines that it was decided to withhold the naval gunfire for fear of causing more casualties from friendly fire than from the enemy. But the attack began at 7:30 that morning.

Minor gains were made that morning, and no indication was given by the Japanese that they were ready to fulfill General Cates's prediction that the Meatgrinder would fall this day. Heavy resistance continued from Minami village, Turkey Knob, and the Amphitheater. But the marines were now in control of Hill 382, and from there they could push to the coast, where the terrain would not so definitely favor the enemy.

But back in the Meatgrinder, forward progress stopped by midafternoon, and even a fifteen-minute artillery barrage staged at 5:00 P.M. did not soften up the enemy. An infantry attack that followed gained less than two hundred yards, and regretfully General Cates ordered the lines secured for the night without having his victory.

That day, however, the reason for the whole bloody effort of the marines on Iwo Jima was made apparent. At 4:30 that morning, as the marines were in their foxholes preparing for the new attack on the Meatgrinder, more than 70 B-29s took off from Saipan for a bombing raid on Japan. Their course took them straight across Iwo Jima about noon, when the fighting for the day at the Meatgrinder was at its height. Most marines did not even look up, and if they did, the overcast mostly covered the high flying B-29s. At 11:30 the B-29s bombed, and after the bombs were gone, the bombardier of the Superfortress *Dinah Might* announced that his bomb doors would not close. Apparently they had frozen open in the high altitude cold. The bomber was otherwise unhurt, having taken only a near miss from Japanese antiaircraft fire.

The pilot throttled back to conserve fuel and headed toward Saipan. There was plenty of fuel to take them home, he said. But strong headwinds and the drag of the open bomb bays slowed the plane, and three hours out from Japan, not quite halfway home, the red light on the fuel tanks began to flash. It was time to switch to the 1,000-gallon reserve fuel tank.

The pilot switched on the changeover valve, but nothing happened. Either the near miss from the Japanese gunners had holed the tank or something had caused the valve to malfunction. In any case there was no fuel to be had from the reserve tanks. The B-29 had fuel only for a half an hour of further flight.

There were two possible options. One was to ditch at sea, and hope that a submarine or a Catalina flying boat or a destroyer would pick them up. Or the pilot could try an emergency landing at Iwo Jima, if the field would take him. No one had yet tried. The pilot decided to give Iwo Jima a call.

The call was taken aboard the command ship *Auburn*, where communications men were still handling everything relating to the airfield. The B-29 gave position, course, and speed, and the airmen on the *Auburn* promised to clear the runway of Airfield No. 1 of bulldozers, and warned the crew to look out for enemy artillery fire and snipers as they came in.

The pilot of the *Dinah Might* brought his Superfortress down low over the island, made two practice passes, and then lined up on the north-south runway of Airfield No. 1. Less than a hundred feet from the ground, the wheels came down. The B-29 landed hard on the packed volcanic sand and bounced twice, but stayed on the runway. The pilot put on the brakes and reversed the thrust of the propellers, and the plane ran the full length of the runway and screeched to a stop at the northern tip. The only casualty was a telephone pole snapped off by the plane's left wing. The wing was not seriously damaged.

The plane swung around and taxied fast toward Mt. Suribachi, because the pilot remembered what the operator had said about snipers and gunfire. Japanese mortar fire came down on the runway, but nowhere near the moving plane. At the end of the runway, the crew tumbled out of the plane, fell to the ground on hands and knees, and kissed the ground.

"What a contrast," said one marine. "Here were men so glad to be on the island that they were kissing it. A mile or so to the north were three marine divisions who thought the place was hell on earth."

The B-29 was on the ground at Iwo for half an hour. Mechanics repaired the fuel transfer valve. The bomb bay doors had closed during the flight. The fliers declined the invitation to spend the night and took off, lest the Japanese open up with

158 IWO JIMA

antiaircraft fire. The pilot took off, banked steeply to the right, and the plane disappeared in a cloud bank.

So the reason for the marine assault on Iwo Jima had now paid off for the first time. One B-29 crew blessed the island and the men who were still fighting for it.

And as the *Dinah Might* disappeared into the clouds, the marines in the Meatgrinder continued to fight and to die, most of them having no idea that the Superfortress had ever landed and taken off.

That night, General Cates had to face the probabilities of the next day. There was no easy way. Every foot of the ground of the Meatgrinder would have to be taken the hard way, by the personal assault of marines on those strong points at Turkey Knob, the Amphitheater, and Minami village. So far, nearly 3,000 marines had been killed and wounded in the Meatgrinder. There would be more.

On the morning of March 4, which was D + 13, the Third Division Twenty-first Regiment was scheduled to attack at 7:30 to go through the Motoyama area and take the high ground overlooking the northern beaches. It was raining. The attack was to be carried out by both the Second Battalion and the Third Battalion, and both of them were slim shadows of their original fighting strength. But General Smith still refused to give General Erskine his Third Marines, the regiment still held in reserve. So these few men would have to try to do the big job. They were exhausted and not very strong, wet from the morning rain and shivering in what seemed to be the cold, although it was 75 degrees Fahrenheit. As soon as they began to move, the familiar sound of the Japanese machine guns and mortars started too. The weather hung down into the ravines, with the visibility less than fifty yards in any direction. Clouds of steam hovered over the ground, and the sulfur hot springs in this area were so close to the surface that fumes assaulted the men almost with the force of gas.

Slowly, raggedly, the marine line moved ahead, through the pelting rain. They were pinned down by Japanese fire. A twenty-minute marine artillery barrage and naval gunfire failed to get the advance going again. They had gained about a hundred yards. Then it was five o'clock and the word came down. "Hold your ground and dig in for the night."

Another day on Iwo Jima had come to an end, and the exhausted marines felt as far from victory as they had been in the beginning.

That day the brass seemed to realize that the marines were on the verge of exhaustion. Plotting on their maps on the command ships, they saw that the marines in two weeks of fighting had progressed to the point they were supposed to have reached, according to plan, on the night of D + 1. General Smith and General Schmidt issued orders that there would be no general attack on March 4, but instead the three divisions would use the time for rest, refitting, and preparing to resume the offensive on March 6.

They needed the rest and they needed the time. The regiments had all lost between 40 and 60 percent of their officers and men. Eleven battalion commanders had fallen, and so many junior officers and noncoms that no attempt was made for a general count. The worst problem was that the fighting teams within the battalions and companies had been broken. Two thousand replacements were on hand, and many of them had already been thrown into the battle. But although these were well-trained marines, they had not served in battle before, and they had not served with the men who would have to depend on them for their lives. They were green, and the only way to ripen them was to take them under fire.

There was a change in the battle scene on March 4. The cooks had spent most of the night preparing hundreds of gallons of hot coffee and fresh donuts and sandwiches, enough for 15,000 marines in the line.

As dawn came, so did the artillery barrages from both sides, but this day there was no attack to follow. Instead the cooks brought up the coffee and prepared food. "Not exactly what you would call room service at the Waldorf," said one marine sergeant, "but it sure beats cold C-rations."

Regimental and battalion commanders merged the half-destroyed units to bring them as close to full strength as possible. The replacements came in new clean uniforms, and

160 IWO JIMA

nervous. Some of them would soon become seasoned veterans. The rest of them would be dead or out of the battle, wounded.

New barrels were fitted to field guns and machine guns. New rifles were issued to the riflemen and new BARs to the automatic riflemen. Medical supplies were replenished, and there were all the items of equipment that a man needed. New flamethrowers came in and the old ones were patched up. The demolitions men got new supplies of satchel charges, and the artillery repaired their field guns and howiters. The tank crews oiled and greased and replaced cannon and tank tracks. On the airfields, the Seabees and engineers worked on the runways. They were in full use of Airfield No. 1, with hospital planes from Saipan taking off every half hour. Army fighter planes arrived to be parked and ready to accompany the B-29s on their missions to Japan. Some men got haircuts. Some went to the movies. Some washed their clothes.

Shortly after 8:30 that morning "Howling Mad" Smith came ashore for an inspection and went into a stormy session with the fighting marines' generals. They demanded that he give them the Third Marines to shore up General Erskine's Third Marine Division. Smith refused again. The fighting generals said that the bringing of 3,000 new men into the line would speed operations and save lives. But General Smith had his orders from Admiral Kelly Turner, who used the excuse that there was no room for more marines on the island. This was selfserving to the nth degree, but that was the way Admiral Kelly Turner was. In the days before Pearl Harbor, he had been one of the most selfserving in the naval high command. As director of Naval Plans in Washington he had effectively prevented Admiral Husband Klimmel from receiving information from Naval Intelligence that would have made it obvious that the Japanese were about to attack Pearl Harbor, and had thus been more responsible than any other figure for the surprise of the attack on Pearl Harbor. Turner, to protect himself, wanted to be sure to have fresh troops to assault Japan, and the only fresh troops available and not committed to Okinawa, the next operation, were the Third Marines. He would not let them go unless virtually every marine on Iwo Jima was shot down. The battle of the generals was fought on the rocky shore of Iwo Jima that day, and the generals who wanted to win the real fight on Iwo Jima lost.

So March 4 was a day of rest for some marines. But not all. The orders that came down from General Schmidt had specified that the marines were to carry out "limited adjustment of positions," and this meant that some marines would have to drive some Japanese out of some positions. It meant more carnage on the day of rest. The Second Battalion of the Twenty-eighth Marines, Chandler Johnson's men, had to fight to adjust their lines, which meant taking care of some bypassed caves and pillboxes overlooking the western shoreline.

In the Third Division's sector, the day was marked by artillery duels between marines and the Japanese. In the south division sector, the marines were busy cleaning out caves and bypassed pillboxes along the southern edge of the Meatgrinder. In the Fifth Division area, the lines had to be straightened along ravines and ridges. Two tanks were knocked out here that day, one by a mine, the other by an antitank gun.

Early in the afternoon, Lieutenant Colonel John Butler, commander of the Third Battalion of the Twenty-seventh Marines, was driving in a jeep with three others, moving slowly on a bumpy road. He stopped at an intersection to take a look at a ridge. The jeep stopped, and an artillery round came in, decapitated Butler, and wounded two of the others in the jeep. On this day of rest, 400 men of the three marine divisions were killed or wounded.

All too often the action went like this:

Two marines approached the cliff and spotted the hidden mouth of a bypassed cave. Gingerly they approached, and came face to face inside with a whole squad of Japanese soldiers. The two marines turned to run, and were shot down by the Japanese. Outside, their fellow marines turned a flamethrower on the cave, and then put a satchel charge in the entrance, sealing the cave, the American dead and the Japanese dead lying together inside.

And as the day came to an end, General Smith went back to his command ship and conferred with Admiral Turner again.

There was no need to discuss the situation about the Third Marines again, because even as "Howling Mad" Smith had been conferring with the fighting generals on Iwo Jima, the transports aboard which the Third Marines were riding had been detached and sent back toward the Marianas, where they would go on garrison duty and start training for the invasion of Japan.

CHAPTER NINETEEN

But a Limited Success

The two-day respite from battle was followed by a renewed assault on March 6, beginning at 7:00 A.M. Naval guns, the artillery, and carrier planes from the escort carriers attacked, dropping clusters of napalm bombs and firing with machine guns and rockets. The firepower exerted was almost equal to that of D Day, except that it was more closely concentrated, and after more than two weeks of fighting the marines and navy had a much better idea of their targets and how to hit them.

More than 130 marine howitzers from eleven artillery battalions fired, first for half an hour on the western half of the island and then for half an hour on the east side. Offshore a battleship and three cruisers fired 14-inch and 8-inch shells along with the three destroyers and two landing craft that also joined in the bombardment. But the results again were a tribute to the strength and care with which General Kuribayashi had built the Iwo Jima defenses. When the marines began the infantry attack, shortly after eight o'clock that morning, the fire from the Japanese was as strong as ever. The barrage and aerial action did not seem to have weakened their defenses at all.

"It was apparent that all the blasting by artillery, naval gunfire, and planes had accomplished little to reduce the enemy's ability and will to resist," said the official report of the Fifth Amphibious Corps that day, "but progressive diminution of enemy artillery had been noticed for several days. It was the mortar and automatic weapons fire that now made every yard of advance so costly."

Or, as one marine put it in marine talk: "All the bombardment did was let the Nips know that we were coming at them again. It stirred them up like a hornet's nest and the sonsabitches were waiting in their caves and bunkers to kill more marines just as they had every goddamned day since we landed."

The Twenty-seventh Marines, and the Twenty-first Marines were to move on the western side of the line, and the Twenty-third Marines and the Twenty-fourth Marines on the eastern side. The Second Battalion of the Twenty-seventh was in place for attack at 5 A.M. That was a long time before the attack was to begin. All it did was give the Japanese a chance to shoot-up the outfit. Mortars landing in the Company E sector of the line killed or wounded thirty-five marines before the jump-off.

When the infantry moved out just after eight o'clock, almost immediately the advance stopped. The area bristled with pillboxes, some of them knocked out earlier but now remanned. Automatic weapons fire spurted from them and from the bunkers and from caves in the hillside. For the Fifth Division, advance was measured in yards, and each yard meant work for flamethrowers, flamethrower tanks, and demolition squads.

On the marine right, the Third Division had easier going. Two platoons of G Company's Second Battalion of the Twenty-first Marines managed to get to the top of a ridge a quarter of a mile from the island's north shore. But there they were pinned down. Lieutenant William Mulvey, the company commander, sent back for help. At the command post, a dozen volunteers set out with flamethrowers and demolitions to rescue the company, but so intense was the Japanese fire that six of the rescuers were killed and two others wounded before they could get to the line.

In this area of the island, the attackers had an additional complication. So many underground hot springs gurgled up that it was virtually impossible to dig foxholes because of the heat and the sulfur fumes. So the marine advance was stopped here as well, after such an easy start. Late in the afternoon Lieutenant Mulvey brought G Company back to the

But a Limited Success   165

line of departure and farther, to positions beyond Motoyama village. Men spent the night in foxholes they had occupied two nights earlier. They had made as much progress as 200 yards in some places, but the cost had been 200 marines killed or wounded.

On the other side of the marine line, two battalions from the Twenty-third Marines and two battalions from the Twenty-fourth Marines comprised the Fourth Division assault force. The leading companies immediately came under heavy fire and were stopped. Fifteen minutes after the attack began, the company commander and a dozen men of Company E of the Twenty-third Marines were killed or wounded. After fifty yards, the attack came to a stop. Late in the afternoon, the company command post was hit by several mortar shells of a new Japanese barrage. The new company commander was wounded, his executive officer killed, and twenty-two enlisted men killed or wounded. When the battalion intelligence officer took over the company, he became its seventh commander since D Day.

The Third Battalion of the Twenty-fourth Marines had it easy, comparatively at least. The area they were hitting was flat enough that they could use tanks. Four flamethrower tanks took the point and the battalion moved up 350 yards that day.

By nightfall, the proof of the argument of the fighting generals against the top brass was shown in the statistics. All three divisions had been reduced to less than half their original fighting capacity. All the replacements on Iwo Jima had now been thrown into the line. Now came the call for rear echelon men: cooks, clerks, truck drivers, carpenters, mechanics, and musicians. There was no one else, since Admiral Turner had insisted that the Third Marines be saved from combat for his future plans, and so they were already 200 miles from Iwo Jima, steaming toward Guam.

So far, the marines had suffered nearly 12,000 casualties. The reporters were now beginning to compare the carnage with that of the Civil War. And as everyone on Iwo Jima knew, it was not over yet by a long shot.

At the end of March 6, General Erskine realized that, as he had feared, the two-day respite had been no substitute for fresh troops. Unless something new were done, the casualty rate would continue as it had, and this seemed to him appalling. He called his commanders together at his command post at the northern end of Airfield No. 1 and proposed a major attack in the darkness before dawn, a surprise assault that he hoped would catch the Japanese napping.

Several officers questioned the wisdom of the operation. It was very risky, particularly since the division was so short on trained officers and noncoms, and the replacements had not really had time to learn the ropes and become truly functioning parts of the combat team.

Nor were the marines trained for night operations, and the terrain in which they were going was alive with places for ambush. "I don't know what the hell will happen, General," said Captain Oscar Salgo, the commander of the division reconnaisance company, "but we'll do our goddamnedest, you can be sure of that." So it was decided that the attempt would be made, and permission was asked from General Schmidt at Fifth Amphibious Corps headquarters. It was granted, and the troops got ready for their first major night assault of the Pacific War.

The southern end of the island gave a picture of reassurance that was not borne out in the north. Motoyama Airfield No. 1 was now looking like a rear echelon fighter field, with aircraft parked all over. The Army Seventh Fighter Command was in place and bringing in more planes each day, P-51s and Black Widow night fighters. Nearly a dozen C-46 transports were on the edges of the runways, having come in with ammunition, medical supplies, and mail. The airfield was still being shelled by the Japanese, but the planes were protected in revetments and by dispersal.

Offshore, the sharply diminished bombardment fleet waited for the end of the battle. The last hospital ship left the island for Guam. From now on, casualties would be evacuated by air.

On Mt. Suribachi, the Seabees were improving the road. When they finished it would be two lanes and thirty-five feet wide with a grade of no more than 10 percent. A luxury highway, some marines snorted.

Suribachi itself continued to have its dangers. There were still Japanese in the caves there, but they were so dispirited and so weak that they spent the days in hiding and came out at night only to search for food and water. One by one they were dying of starvation.

As the Japanese of Suribachi emerged from their caves after midnight to forage for food, two companies of the Third Battalion of the Ninth Marines were preparing to move into the line to make the spearhead of the American night attack. Their objective would be Hill 362 C, 250 yards to their southeast. It was the last Japanese stronghold between the Third Division and the north shore. By 3:30 they were getting into position.

It was raining steadily and the night was black. The company commanders tried to find points of orientation, but they were hard to see. For once it was quiet along the line, and the marines moved as quietly as possible. At 4:50 all star shells and other illumination of the front stopped, but at five o'clock a destroyer mistakenly fired a star shell. For once, the marines were very glad when the shell was almost immediately burned out by the downpour and the friendly blackness returned.

Just before five o'clock, the marine artillery began firing smoke shells, to screen the advance. The attackers crawled forward. It seemed that they had achieved their objective and surprised the enemy. They crawled ahead for half an hour without response from the enemy, until a machine gun spoke up. Almost immediately the gun was put out of action by a flamethrower. And the marines passed through the lines. They had not suffered a casualty, for the first time in many days of attacking.

General Erskine began to get encouraging reports. Radio silence was broken and the news was spread around, the good news of success. General Erskine beamed. "I had a hunch it would work," he told his intelligence officers. "We caught the bastards asleep, just as I thought we would."

The report came that the company was on top of Hill 362 C. It seemed too good to be true. And it was. When the darkness began to evaporate, the commander of the Third Battalion found that his company was on top of hill 331, not Hill 362 C. So the marines had taken their hill, but it was the wrong hill.

At least they were going in the right direction, and Hill 362 C was only 250 yards ahead of them. The marines resumed their attack. But by this time the Japanese were thoroughly aroused, and they were fighting back. Some of their positions that had been bypassed came to life and began to throw fire into the marines from the sides and back. It was the same story as before. It was late afternoon before Hill 362 C was finally captured.

The story was much the same in the areas of the First and Second Battalions. Both gained several hundred yards before the heavy fighting began. But when it did begin, it was the story of bypassed Japanese coming out to fight from the rear and the flanks, and riflemen being cut off and cut to ribbons.

Companies E and F of the Second Battalion were surrounded in the area that came to be known as Cushman's Pocket, named after the battalion commander. They were stuck in this declivity. Tanks and riflemen tried to extricate them, but without success.

The Company B commander watched his men fall and became throughly pessimistic about the future. By midafternoon, he had lost thirty-two killed and twenty wounded, and was 400 yards out in front of the line. The company had lost contact with the attack. Its commander, Second Lieutenant John Leims, knew that something had to be done if any of them were to come out alive. If they were left out all night, they were finished. He decided to go for help. He started back, under the cover of a boulder, but was spotted by the Japanese. He began to dodge and run, crawling sometimes, snaking his way along, and then darting behind cover. He was under heavy fire, but he was not hit. His trip across the four hundred yards took ten minutes. He made it unharmed, with mortar shells bursting around him and machine guns kicking up dust at his feet and narrowly missing his head. He got to the battalion command post and showed them on an aerial photograph where his company was holed up. He did not use a map. The maps were outdated and the artillery and mortars

But a Limited Success   171

Sergeant Josephy made his way up front to the area where the First Battalion companies were in action. He came to a lone marine guarding a pile of rations, and the marine showed him a dud Japanese shell that had just come in over his shoulder and skidded across the pile without exploding. It was one of those minor miracles that marines blessed.

The sergeant then went up toward the company area, about 200 yards ahead, zigzagging across open ground, hearing the sound of a Nambu machine gun. He found A and B Companies.

"Able and Baker companies were dug into foxholes among the sand dunes and bushes across the field. The foxholes were close together around a knocked out Jap antitank gun that poked through a concrete fort built between two dunes. The men looked as though they had just come from a hard-fought football game. They leaned against the sides of the foxholes, exhausted and breathing heavily. Their eyes were wide open and staring, as if they could not forget the terrible sights they had seen. I recognized many friends and tried talking to them, but it was useless. They looked through me. Their answers made no sense. Their minds wandered. One man tried to ask me how the battle was going. He couldn't get his question out. He finished half the sentence, then repeated the last words over and over, like a man falling asleep. But he wasn't drowsing. His mind just wouldn't function."

Josephy discovered that Able Company was down to one commissioned officer, a captain. A lieutenant and some men from the Third Battalion came up. They were picking up their dead, they said, and the lieutenant looked at the captain and observed that they were going back into the line again in the afternoon. It wasn't really a question. The captain confirmed it. The lieutenant sighed and motioned to the enlisted men with him to follow him as he picked his way across the clearing toward the rear. The Nambu machine gun opened fire again. They found the dead and carried them back on stretchers to the revetment aid station. It took them several trips.

That afternoon, the First and Third Battalions were supposed to go into action again, but the orders never came to move out.

172 IWO JIMA

So in the evening they dug in again for another night on Iwo.

"The night in the sand was hideous," wrote Sergeant Josephy. "Land crabs crawled among the bushes and down the dunes, scraping along the ashes and sounding like Japanese slithering toward our foxholes. Illuminating flares hung overhead, casting weird moving shadows across the terrain. The Japs threw mortar shells and our artillery answered, and the sky was filled with the whirring breath of missiles sailing back and forth above our heads. Every so often a terrific crash sounded close by, where a mortar shell fell among us. We dozed in turns, trying to ignore the clamor, which in our fitful dreams sounded like someone banging doors in a house in which we were trying to sleep. The doors were all around us, upstairs and downstairs, in the same room and on the other side of the house. Suddenly someone slammed a door in our face."

He awoke with a start. The banging was still going on and sand was coming in on them from the lip of the foxhole. It was in their mouths and ears. They all shifted position and tried to sleep on. The man guarding their foxhole didn't notice the stirring. He lay silently against the edge of the foxhole, staring into the night.

That day's predawn attack had proved to be a qualified success. In Cushman's Pocket it had failed, and the Japanese remained in total control. But the capture of all that ground in the beginning, even though it was the wrong ground, had proved to lay the basis for success, for later the marines discovered that the ground they had taken so easily in the night, had been the most heavily fortified in the area. And in the end they had taken Hill 362 C, although it had cost 600 men dead and wounded. But it was the last remaining major obstacle to the drive to the northern shore and in the center of the island.

CHAPTER TWENTY

A Little Help

The next day, the order came to the First and Third Battalions of the Twenty-first Marines to move up. The Ninth Marines, who had been in the line for two days, were exhausted.

The Third Battalion of the Twenty-first moved toward the northern end of Airfield No. 2, to attack the high ground. On the right, the Third Battalion prepared to attack across entirely different terrain. The First Battalion faced sand dunes and flatland. The Third faced ravines and gulleys, ridges, and crags. It was a landscape that would remind a later generation of the moon.

That morning, the artillery delivered a rolling barrage, from the guns of the cruisers and destroyers and all the artillery the marines could muster on the shore. For forty-five minutes the guns crashed, then the fire lifted and the men move up 100 yards. With fixed bayonets and grenades, the infantry began to attack.

The barrage had accomplished something. On the left, the First Battalion moved forward 200 yards with virtually no opposition before the Japanese could recover. Then, when the Japanese began to fire again, the marines sought cover, and began attacking pillboxes and individual Japanese positions.

Flamethrower and demolitions men came up to attack the caves in the rocks. The flamethrower man would go in and burn the cave, the demolitions men would hurl grenades or demolitions charges, and the cave would be declared all cleared out. That was true for a few hours. But after the hours passed,

174 IWO JIMA

the marines who came back that way again found the caves still spouting fire and the Japanese back, having retreated into the labyrinth of caves and tunnels and returned. As always on Iwo Jima, the progress was slow and it was mostly made by the infantry, cave by cave and pillbox by pillbox. That night, the attack ended and the men settled down in holes several yards ahead of the ridge. But that night, too, the Japanese moved back through their tunnels to get behind the marines. Next morning, all those positions cleared the day before began to erupt fire again. An aid station was established by the First Battalion at the end of the ridge. But the Japanese were all around it. Sergeant Josephy and a corpsman watched as four stretcher bearers came down the road with a wounded man on their stretcher. They moved directly into the Japanese fire.

"The corpsman cupped his hands over his mouth, to try to warn the stretcher bearers, but there was too much noise and they couldn't hear him. The Japanese began to fire at them. They ran faster. Then a bullet hit one of them in the leg. He looked around wildly and crashed to the ground. The stretcher spilled on top of him. The men in front tripped as they tried to hold onto the stretcher. The Japs kept shooting into the group. The wounded stretcher bearer jumped up again and grabbed his end of the litter. He started to drag the stretcher along, but dropped it. The man on the stretcher hung half over it, his head and shoulders dragging along the ground. The other men half crawled and half ran with the stretcher until they reached the rocks. The wounded stretcher bearer loped after them. When he reached the shelter he fell again. It was a miracle that he had been able to stay on his feet, for the bullet had laid open his calf as if it had been hit by a meat cleaver. The man on the stretcher was stone dead, one of the bullets from the ridge had hit him in the skull."

The battalion called for tanks. When they appeared, the men started the step-by-step process of cleaning out the ridge all over again. But there were too many caves and too many holes. They called for flamethrower tanks, which came up. The flamethrowers began sending long tongues of fire into the caves and down the tunnels. The marines could hear the Japanese yelling. A few Japanese rushed out, on fire. The marines shot them or beat out the flames and took them prisoner. Then they began to hear the muffled sounds of explosion inside the hillside. They knew then that some of the Japanese were blowing themselves up with grenades.

The flamethrowers paused for a break. A marine stood up and looked around. There was no firing from the area. A Japanese came out of a hole and raised his hands. The marines stood behind the rocks and waved him to come on. He indicated that there were more who would surrender. The marines motioned them to come. Soon about forty Japanese came out of these holes. They said they were Koreans who had been forced to stay in the caves. They also said that the area was now quiet. Almost all of the Japanese here had either been burned to death by the flamethrowers or had committed suicide.

The marines had the ridge, and they peered and poked among the rocks from hole to hole, examining the dead bodies. An officer made notes to bring up demolition crews and seal up the holes and caves to make certain all was over here. But before the demolition men could come up, more Japanese appeared from the caves and tunnels beneath the ridge, and the ridge line was a fighting ground once again. It was here on this day that Sergeant Reid Carlos Chamberlain, one of the most popular men of the regiment, and one of its heroes, was killed.

Sergeant Chamberlain was already a legendary figure. He had been on Corregidor in the first days of the war, and on the night of May 6, 1942, just before the surrender of the American forces, he had found an abandoned boat on the beach there and managed to reach Mindanao, where he joined the guerilla movement led by Colonel Wendell Fertig, and was commissioned a lieutenant in the U.S. Army. Two years later, Chamberlain was taken out of the Philippines by submarine and brought to Washington to sell war bonds. General Vandegrift of the Marine Corps delivered the Army Distinguished Service Medal that Chamberlain had won and offered him a commission in the Marine Corps. But Chamberlain went back into marine service as a sergeant and was assigned to Company A of the

Twenty-first Marines. He was serving as a runner in this battle for the ridge line and had been for two days, making his way across the disputed territory between the marine command post and the front line. On this second day, he was running up to A Company, and he asked Sergeant Josephy, the correspondent, to accompany him. They crossed the clearing that a few minutes earlier had been so quiet and apparently cleared of Japanese sniper fire. They stuck to the ridge line for protection and were picking their way along the rocks when shots ran out. Sergeant Chamberlain drew his automatic pistol and looked around. Then Sergeant Josephy heard another shot and a thud. He and several others went on, but when Chamberlain did not appear they came back and found his body. He had been shot through the head by a sniper. The furious marines poured a hail of fire into all the holes in the area, and the sniping stopped again. They tried to find flamethrowers to sear out the holes, but the flamethrowers were all busy. They went to the Ninth Marines contingent that was moving up to the ridge and told them that the ridge line was still full of Japanese. The captain considered the problems, but decided to was too late in the day to mount an an attack on the ridge, so he posted guards to keep any marines from wandering off there, and set up the perimeter.

That night, the Japanese came out of their holes and tried to launch an attack. The marine guards saw them and began picking them off with automatic fire. Some were killed and others retreated into the holes. On top of the ridge, the marines could hear the thud of grenades as some of the Japanese blew themselves up, committing suicide when they realized they were trapped. Then at about midnight, an enormous explosion ripped the ridge. Huge boulders were scattered, and poured down into the marine foxholes. Some men were hurled into the air and fell back, and some were buried in the foxholes. There was more explosion and fire. The marines dug themselves out and moved down the ridge to safer locations. They took position behind the rocks and waited. Now they knew what had happened. The Japanese had blown their ammunition dump beneath the ridge, in mass suicide.

Some Japanese began to come out, ready to fight. One marine saw two of them with antipersonnel mines tied around the waists, and killed them before they could move. Some Japanese tried to struggle out of the tunnels, to be buried in landslides, with arms and legs sticking out from the rocks.

Marines looked around the ridge. It was not really a ridge any more, but the wreckage of one. When daylight came and the marines poked around among the holes, they discovered that the Japanese had used aerial bombs and land mines to blow the ridge to bits. In all this, while many men were buried and knocked about, all were rescued and only one serious American casualty had been incurred.

The third day was spent trying to seal up all the holes, caves, and cracks in what remained of the old Japanese defenses. But at the end of the day, many caves were still unsealed, and the marines gave up the job and moved on.

"We ought to put up a sign that says 'pass at your own risk', " one marine joked.

Two days later, this area was considered to be in the rear. A supply outfit moved in and set up tents and galleys, built a motor pool parking lot for vehicles, and began to supply the troops up front. That afternoon, a jeep and trailer set out for the front lines with coffee and donuts. As it passed the remains of the ridge, it was fired on by a field gun. The jeep driver stepped on the gas pedal and sped out of the area. On the way back, he was shot at again. Later jeep ambulance drivers and other vehicle drivers reported being fired on. Then a tank was hit, and the crew jumped out and took cover. They came back to the supply unit and reported that an antitank gun was somewhere up there. Another tank was sent up, it waited behind the rocks until the Japanese gun fired at a vehicle and showed its position. Then the tank's 75mm gun blasted the Japanese position, Automatic riflemen came up to take care of any Japanese survivors. They found the wreckage of a 47mm antitank gun, which had survived the whole incident of three days on the ridge.

And the story of the ridge did not end. There were still a number of Japanese soldiers inside that hill. Riflemen and machine gunners emerged from time to time to fire at the marines. They were very careful and only appeared when there was something to shoot at.

This became apparent a day or so later, when a telephone lineman was stringing wires between poles and was shot through the head. Two cooks were shot in the arms. A mortar platoon was pinned down by a Japanese machine gun.

The area quieted down again, and new marines became nonchalant about the ridge. One day, an officer was having his hair cut, and he and the barber were sent scuttling for cover by a fusillade of small arms fire. Marines came up from time to time to work the area over again with automatic rifles, flamethrowers, and demolition charges. But on D + 25, a Japanese sniper shot a navy corpsman through the ear on this ridge.

On D + 16, the Fifth Division's Twenty-sixth Marines began an attack at dawn, without any artillery support. This came about not because they were trying for surprise, but because they had run out of artillery shells in the previous day's bombardment. But the effects were salutary. The Japanese were surprised and the marines fought against a difficult defense position built around a hill. Suddenly this hill blew up, in the same manner that the ridge had done. In this case, the Japanese had blown their command post. But the results were not as they had been on the ridge line. Fifty marines of the Twenty-sixth Regiment were killed or wounded by the blast. What the Japanese did here became more common day after day, as the Japanese units saw they had lost the battle.

Colonel Liversedge's Twenty-eighth Marines had a little easier going that morning of D + 16. They moved along the western shoreline of the island against light resistance. The terrain was difficult, steep, and rocky as they moved toward Kitano Point. Destroyers paved the way for them with a barrage of fire. The marines progressed about 500 yards that morning. But sniper fire, grenades, and mortars caused casualties here, too.

On the Fourth Division front, the action began at night in the early hours of D + 16, as the Japanese infiltrators searched for weak spots in the marine line. The first raid aroused the marines, and it was wiped out before it could get started in

Captain Headley's Third Battalion sector. Then, an hour later, the Japanese began probing the First Battalion's sector and a two-hour firefight began along a front of 200 yards. The battle was lighted by starshells, and the fighting was sometimes hand-to-hand before the Japanese were subdued. About fifty Japanese moved about, some of them jumping into foxholes and engaging in combat to the death with the marines. The marines used every weapon at hand, including rocks. A dozen Japanese who were hugging the sides of a ravine on their way down were illuminated by a flare and killed in a hail of rifle and machine gun fire. When dawn came, the marines counted fifty bodies, but thirteen marines had also been killed in this fighting.

When the bodies were examined, something was learned about the enemy's situation. Many of the Japanese were carrying more than one canteen, and all of them were dry. Others had no ammunition with which to reload their rifles. So they were short of water and ammunition. The only weapons of two of the infiltrators were antipersonnel mines they had strapped around their waists. So they were also short of grenades.

But short of conventional weapons or not, the Japanese were still very dangerous. The night infiltration had been all wiped out, and the marines were waiting for the day's action to begin, when one of those huge Japanese mortars made one of its infrequent connections. The missile struck in the middle of the command post of the Twenty-third Marines Second Battalion, killing the communications officer, wounding the commanding officer, his executive and operations officers, and the battalion adjutant and two clerks. The battalion was taken over by the regimental executive officer, but when the Fourth Division attack started at 7:30, the battalion was ready to go.

This day, they found that the night's activity had taken some of the starch out of the enemy, and Japanese fire power around Turkey Knob was far less strong than it had been before. Gains of the day in terms of territory were not very great, but casualties were lighter than usual. For the first time, Turkey Knob seemed to be weakening.

That day, the Third Division came almost to the point of breakthrough to the coast in the center of the line. The Fifth

Division closed in on Kitano Point on the west coast. General Schmidt could now see the end of the struggle for control of the island, although perhaps he could not say just when the day would come on which the Japanese would be completely subdued in their underground hideouts. As he now suspected, that would mean when all of them were dead. And there was still plenty of Japanese life in Cushman's Pocket, for the Third Division, around Turkey Knob for the Fourth Division, and in the Kuribayashi headquarters in the northwest.

CHAPTER TWENTY-ONE

Pressure

On D + 17, the First Battalion of the Twenty-seventh Marines moved out on the Fifth Division front. Company E was the spearhead, and it ran immediately into heavy fire from machine guns, rifles, and mortars. Despite such opposition, the company advanced two hundred yards that morning. The commander, Lieutenant Jack Lummus, was knocked down by the concussion from a grenade and then charged the position from which it had come and killed the occupants with his submachine gun. He was wounded in the shoulder by another grenade, but after taking cover for a moment he charged still another position and killed its three occupants. Then he motioned to the men of the company to come up. They followed twenty yards behind as he charged forward. Then came a great explosion, and when the smoke cleared it appeared that Lieutenant Lummus was standing in a hole. Both his legs had been blown off by a land mine. But he was still shouting at his men: "Come on. Come on. Don't stop now! Keep coming, godamn it!"

The men swept forward 300 yards, overwhelming foxholes and pillboxes, and blasting caves and sniper pits. Some of them had tears in their eyes as they passed their mortally wounded commanding officer, but they were inspired, and they moved swiftly and ruthlessly to kill the enemy that had killed him.

Lieutenant Lummus was taken back to the Fifth Division hospital and given transfusions. But the doctors could not stop the bleeding. He lived for several hours, conscious all the time, and laughing and joking with the doctors, and then he died. Posthumously, he received the twentieth Medal of Honor of the Iwo Jima campaign. And as he died, his men were still advancing. They made another two hundred yards that afternoon and reached the last ridge overlooking the ocean at Kitano Point.

On the Fifth Division front, the Second Battalion also moved forward that day. They were caught in a storm of fire. Private First Class James LaBelle won the Medal of Honor that day too, when he fell on a grenade that otherwise would have killed several marines and took the explosion with his body alone. The Third Division fought again at Cushman's Pocket. Artillery fired on the pocket for ten minutes before their attack, and then tanks came forward firing into the caves and pillboxes. At the end of the day the Third Division had advanced 300 yards, and was about to split the island at the top center.

The Fourth Division kept up the pressure to wipe out the resistance around Turkey Knob. That was all that was left of the Meatgrinder, but it was still grinding. At the end of the day, it looked as though the Japanese might be finished in this area on the next day, if there were enough marines and enough firepower to finish the job. As night fell and General Cates considered his casualties, he wondered. The replacement pool had gone dry, and now the final pool of clerks and bakers and truck drivers was drying up. There was only so much attrition that a marine division could stand without reinforcement, and General Cates knew that his division and the other two were rapidly reaching that critical point, with no reinforcements in sight.

On D + 18, Cushman's Pocket continued to be the strong spot of the Japanese defense. Again the assault was preceded here by naval gunfire and artillery fire from the marines' guns. But again, some marines wondered why the navy and the artillery had wasted the shells. The fire from Cushman's Pocket indicated that the strong points were untouched.

That morning, the tanks made some advances, but the first Sherman was knocked out by Japanese satchel charges, and the tanks behind were slowed. The offensive lost its steam, and by midafternoon it was stopped altogether again.

The Twenty-first's First Battalion had sent a patrol around the front and driven to the cliffs that overlook Iwo Jima's north shore. They had met only sporadic resistance, and had not had any real difficulty in making that last move.

On the cliff, they stood looking down at the waves lapping on the beach. They went down the cliff and past knocked-out bunkers and empty caves. There was not a sound from the enemy, not a sign of a living thing. The men got to the beach and some took off their shoes and waded or just washed their feet, and some scooped up water and splashed themselves.

Most of the twenty-seven-man patrol played on the beach for a while. Lieutenant Paul Connally, the commander of the patrol, was on the radio talking to regiment. He knew that they had made an important breakthrough, as important as the capture of Mt. Suribachi. The Third Division had reached the island's northernmost point. The Japanese defenses were now split into two pockets.

Regiment ordered Lieutenant Connally to bring back a canteen of sea-water for General Erskine, and so a canteen was filled. But while they were playing in the surf, the Japanese had been setting up mortars and retraining them on the marines. Before they left, the beach shells began to fall, and seven of the marines were wounded. The others carried them up to the cliff above the beach, and there they dug in for the night. The general would have to wait for his seawater.

When they were dug in, Lieutenant Connally looked over his command: nineteen able-bodied men and seven wounded. When his company had landed on Iwo, his First Battalion was more than a thousand men and his A Company had numbered four hundred men. Now only three of the original A company were left to hit the north shore, and all the others were replacements.

Later that night, he sent the canteen of seawater back to General Erskine's command post by runner. When the general received it, he was going over the casualty figures, and the symbolism of the canteen gave him pause. It had cost the Third

184 IWO JIMA

Division 3,563 men killed, wounded, and missing, or more than half its original assault force, to get from the invasion point to the north shore of Iwo Jima.

The night of D + 18 also happened to be the night of March 8. The eighth day of every month was commemorated by the Japanese to remind the nation that the Great Pacific War had begun on December 8, 1941. The Japanese newspapers all ran the Imperial Rescript of declaration of war on that day, and the Japanese government observed the memory of the event. On this eighth day, Admiral Ichimaru sent a thousand naval troops out in the darkness of night to infiltrate the lines of the Fourth Marine Division. They were full of fighting spirit but very badly armed. Some of them carried bamboo spears and others had only land mines for weapons.

The Japanese moved first against Company E of the Twenty-third Marines. They came down a ravine, moving slowly and steadily. Some of them carried stretchers, and shouted "Corpsman! Corpsman!" as they came. Some stretcher bearers penetrated to within ten yards of the Second Battalion command post before the marines realized who they were. Then the alarm was sounded, and the whole area became a battle zone.

This was a real *banzai* attack, something Admiral Ichimaru had wanted to stage for a long time. Shouts of "*banzai*," and "*totsugeki shite!*" ("Charge!") rang through the air. The marines responded with rifle, machine gun, and automatic rifle fire, and began throwing grenades. Screaming and brandishing their weapons, the Japanese came on, scores of them falling to the marine fusillade, but scores more getting through to Company E and other units to wage hand-to-hand combat in the foxholes. Company E alone used 500 grenades that night, and 200 rounds of 60mm mortar ammunition, 1,200 star shells, and 20,000 rounds of rifle and machine gun bullets.

One by one, the Japanese were wiped out until by daybreak, when the attack waned, about two hundred of those still alive managed to get back to their own lines and into the caves and holes that led to the tunnels. The casualties had been heavy. The marines counted 784 dead Japanese. They had ninety men killed and 257 wounded.

Mopping up continued until noon. One captured Japanese, when interrogated, turned out to be a navy pilot. His orders from the island naval command had been to make his way to Airfield No. 1, steal a B-29, and fly it back to Japan. He had no idea of how to fly a B-29 and believed that there were some on the island.

Other Fourth Division units continued the push across to the eastern shore. They quelled the resistance at Turkey Knob and moved past it. That night, when the marines dug in and prepared their perimeter they could look down from their positions on the ridge line and see the ocean lapping at the foot of the cliff.

That day, Admiral Turner had left Iwo Jima for Guam in his command ship, the *Eldorado*, taking most of the remaining warships with him. There was no ceremony, no encouraging message to the marines, nothing. The job was not finished, but Turner wanted to get back to Guam and prepare for the invasion of Okinawa, which was only half a month away. The naval air force left as well. Admiral Mitscher was long gone, as was the bulk of the carriers, but the carrier *Enterprise* and six escort carriers had remained. Now they too went away, and the air support of the island devolved to the Army Air Force fighter planes on Airfield No. 1.

Command of the invasion forces was left with Rear Admiral Harry Hill. There was not much left to command, just the cruisers *Salt Lake City* and *Tuscaloosa*, and several destroyers. They were left to carry out fire missions on request of the marines.

Two thousand army soldiers came ashore on Iwo Jima that day. The marine on Suribachi who had prepared his cave for the army was to have tenants at last. They would take over the garrison from the marines, just as soon as the Japanese garrison was eliminated. That day, 334 B-29s left the Marianas bound for Tokyo on a new sort of mission. Lieutenant General Curtis LeMay had convinced General Arnold that the Twentieth Air Force was wasting its efforts on high-level bombing directed at the Japanese aircraft industry. The way to force the Japanese out of the war, he declared, was to burn them out, and he proposed that the B-29s switch from high-level bombing to low-level firebombing. This was to be the first great fire raid. As it turned out, it was a spectacular success. The B-29s arrived after midnight, over a Tokyo that was experiencing very high winds. They dropped their clusters of fire bombs, designed to burn up the Japanese wooden and paper houses. The fires started and were spread by the wind until a fire storm began, with winds of a hundred miles an hour, carrying flames as much as a quarter of mile and starting new fires. Sixteen square miles of Tokyo were burned out before daybreak, and the Sumida River was choked with the corpses of the drowned and burned to death who had sought shelter here from the dreadful fires. No one will ever know how many people died in the night's flames. A figure of 84,000 was given, but the total could have been twice that high. Since the bombing of Tokyo had begun, many people had fled the city, but many had not. The keeping of records, so meticulous in the past, was abandoned, and so no one knew how many people were in Tokyo that night, and how many were affected. Many of the bodies were burned to ash, and many were washed out to sea.

The marines still faced heavy fighting on Iwo Jima, particularly in the Fifth Division area. Here the terrain was up and down, with caves and holes everywhere, and these were manned mostly by the naval forces who were determined to die fighting to the last man. In the next forty-eight hours the Fifth Division would fight long and hard to gain fifty yards.

The main obstacle, the marines learned was a long low ridge that jutted out from Kitano Point. The Twenty-seventh Marines First and Second Battalions moved onto this ridge just after daybreak. After the advance bogged down, Lieutenant Colonel Justin Duryea of the First Battalion and Lieutenant Colonel John Antonelli of the Second Battalion got together to plan how they could get the advance going. They were going forward to look over the prospects when their vehicle hit a land mine. Both were seriously wounded and put out of the battle.

That day the area got its name, "The Gorge," which would rank in marine annals with the Meatgrinder and Cushman's Pocket.

Fifteen minutes after the attack started, Platoon Sergeant Joseph Julian's platoon was pinned down by intersecting machine gun fire from several caves. Julian squirmed his way fifty yards into no-man's-land, and attacked a pillbox with grenades. Two grenades did it for the four men inside. Then he saw a machine gun a few yards away. Before the gunner could turn it on him, he leaped behind a boulder and emptied his carbine into the cave, killing two more Japanese and silencing the machine gun. He went back to the marine line for a satchel of demolitions, a bandolier of rifle ammunition, and a bazooka. He told the other men of his platoon to stay put while he wiped out some more Japanese. That was the last the platoon heard of him for three hours. In the interim, he had wiped out four more enemy positions. Then he was hit by machine gun fire and died instantly. The Fifth Division had another Medal of Honor winner.

The Fifth Division that day looked down on Kitano Point. It had driven five miles up the western shore of the island. Its losses were 4,292 men killed, wounded, and missing.

By this time, the Third Marine Division had completed its mission, except for fighting that continued in Cushman's Pocket and by Japanese in bypassed positions. The Fourth Marine Division had finished off the Meatgrinder with the last fighting around Turkey Knob. So it seemed that it must be all over on Iwo Jima.

But was it?

There was more to come.

CHAPTER TWENTY-TWO

The Waste of the Azusa Unit

Since the first of the year, Admiral Soemu Toyoda, the commander of the Japanese Combined Fleet, had nurtured a dream. He would wipe out the strength of the American carrier fleet by a daring blow at the fleet when it was replenishing at Ulithi, the American forward naval base. His dream was called the Tan Operation.

The problem was that the mission had to be one way, for Japan did not have a bomber capable of flying that distance and returning without refuelling, and Japan had now lost all the string of island bases that used to connect her with the South Pacific. After the single *kamikaze* mission of early March, the Japanese in Japan had written off Iwo Jima and concentrated their air forces in the home islands for the next invasion, which they expected to come at Taiwan, on the China coast, Japan proper, or Okinawa. But the strike at Ulithi was something else, a defiant venture that could turn the war around, Admiral Toyoda believed. If the planes of the special unit, called the Azusa Unit, could cripple the American carrier fleet, then the invasions would have to come to an end, and the Americans should be ready to talk peace on terms the Japanese could accept.

By the end of the first week in March, the Azusa unit was ready, twenty-four Ginga bombers, called "Frances" by the Americans, twin-engined bombers with long range, and capable

The Waste of the Azusa Unit

of carrying an 800-kilogram bomb, which is what they would use in this attack on the carriers. They were waiting for word that the American carrier fleet had returned from its forays against Japan and Iwo Jima and was anchored in Ulithi. The word came that the ships were seen moving toward Ulithi, and on March 8, the Azusa unit was moved down to Kanoya air base, the headquarters of Admiral Matome Ugaki, who would supervise this operation. He was charged with the defense of the southern area of Japan, and his Kanoya airbase was the farthest south and closest to Ulithi.

On the night of March 9, Ugaki staged an impressive going-away celebration for the young men who were going out to give their lives to strike such a brave blow for Japan. A special dinner was arranged for them featuring *fugu*, the Japanese blowfish that is such a delicacy. The liver of the *fugu* is poisonous to humans, so *fugu* cooks must be specially licensed. Admiral Ugaki's chief of staff was a *fugu* expert and a licensed cook. So this special feast was prepared. Admiral Ugaki made a speech extolling the virtues of the Azusa unit and there were toasts in *sake* far into the night. Next morning the young men, dressed in their flying clothes and with *hachimaki* (headbands) proclaiming the sacred nature of their mission, came to the airfield. There were traditional toasts in *sake*, the admiral made another speech, and the Azusa unit took off.

The whole mission was neatly managed. One flying boat left Kagoshima Bay at three o'clock in the morning for weather reconnaissance. Four land-based bombers left Kanoya an hour and a half later to patrol ahead of the main force and keep them out of trouble. Four flying boats left Kagoshima at 7:30 to guide the main force to Ulithi. This main force of 24 bomb-laden planes left shortly afterward, and Admiral Ugaki waved them off the Nagoya airfield.

But later that day, a reconnaissance flying boat flying over Ulithi reported only one carrier in Ulithi, and based on this report, the mission was called back. The fliers returned to Kanoya, worn out from the tension and the strain of the flight, plus the heavy weight of the realization that their sacrificial attempt had come to naught and that it must all be done over again. Within twenty-four hours, the signal came that the carriers had indeed arrived at Ulithi, and the planes were put in the air again. This second mission had its problems. The land-based bombers and flying boats to go ahead got mixed up and off schedule. Of the twenty-four planes that had left Kanoya that morning, thirteen developed engine trouble and had to drop out. The remaining eleven planes made it to Ulithi, although they got lost. They found Yap, however, and then were able to set a course for Ulithi, and came in at dusk. All eleven planes announced that they were making their suicidal plunges against the enemy carriers.

And the results?

Nothing. Absolutely nothing. Eleven twin-engined bombers with their crews, eleven 800-kilogram bombs, and nothing.

There were no observation planes to report what had happened, and all the Japanese had were the radio reports and the report of the reconnaissance plane the next day that flew off Ulithi and found no damaged ships.

As for the Americans, they reported nothing. And after the war was ended, in his mammoth *History of U.S. Naval Operations in World War II* Admiral Samuel Eliot Morison reported on all damage to all American ships throughout the war, but for the incident of March 11 at Ulithi there was no report. It was as if it had never happened. Admiral Toyoda's dream had come to nothing at all.

CHAPTER TWENTY-THREE

And the Fighting Went On and On

March 14 was D + 23. The fighting began at dawn and continued until dusk. The Japanese were holding out in The Gorge, in Cushman's Pocket, and around Turkey Knob. If a marine in those areas was asked, how was it going he would say "lousy" or "the Japs just keep coming."

Or he might be wounded, and lying there waiting for the shock to wear off and the pain to begin. Or he might be dead.

What he was *not* doing was celebrating.

But there was celebrating was going on—at Guam. There, Admiral Nimitz had declared victory on Iwo Jima. It was official. The battle was over.

Victory?

Two thousand Japanese were still fighting, living in the tunnels of the island, emerging on the surface like moles to fight. And if they were not killed, they went back below the surface and came out again and again and again.

At 9:30 on the morning of March 14, way down south on the island, about two hundred yards north of Mt. Suribachi, in a burned-out bunker, the ceremonies began.

An honor guard of twenty-four riflemen stood at parade rest. They were not dressed in the red, gold, and blue marine dress uniforms, but in faded dungarees that they had washed the night before. They faced generals—Smith, Schmidt, Cates, Rockey, and Erskine. Admiral Turner had come back for the celebration and stood with Admiral Hill. General Chaney of the army stood waiting to take over command of the island.

They all stood there as an officer read Admiral Nimitz's proclamation that Iwo Jima had been occupied and was now to be governed by the American military.

As they stood there, they could hear the noise of the artillery firing on Cushman's Pocket, where the Japanese did not know that they were now under the command of the American military government.

"All powers of government are vested in me as military governor and will be exercised by subordinate commanders under my direction. All persons will obey promptly the orders given under my authority. Offenses against the forces of occupation will be severely punished."

When the reading was over, a three-man color guard stepped off eighty paces to an 80-foot flagstaff built in concrete atop a demolished Japanese bunker. The color guard ceremoniously unfolded the United States flag and ran it up the staff as a bugler sounded colors. The flag on Mt. Suribachi was lowered, the honor guard presented arms, and Iwo Jima became U.S. territory.

But nobody notified General Kuribayashi, and his guns continued to fire on the marines.

In Washington, President Roosevelt was on Capitol Hill reporting to Congress on the Yalta meeting with Prime Minister Churchill and Premier Stalin.

"The Japs know what it means that 'the marines have landed'," he said to thunderous applause, "and I think I may add that the situation is well in hand." There was more thunderous applause from the congressmen and the senators.

But nobody told Colonel Tom Wornham, commander of the Twenty-seventh Marines. What they did tell him was that the casualties of his Twenty-seventh Marines had become so heavy that the regiment no longer existed as a fighting instrument, and that day it was pulled out of the battle and never fought again.

The generals and the chaplains dedicated the cemeteries American P-51 Mustang fighter planes roared on and off th

And the Fighting Went On and On

runways carrying out close air support missions for the marines on the northern part of the island.

Dedicating the Third Marine Division cemetery, General Erskine said:

"What was in doubt in all our minds was whether there would be any of us left to dedicate our cemetery at the end, or whether the last marine would die knocking out the last Japanese gun and gunner."

The last Japanese gun and gunner were still out there. Perhaps it was this gunner who cut off Major William Tumbelston's left arm that day.

The ceremonies were complete, and the army could now take over garrison duty. The world could forget about Iwo Jima. Officially the battle was won. The cruisers *Salt Lake City* and *Tuscaloosa* sailed away to get ready for the invasion of Okinawa. Six destroyers remained on station. Their major mission was to light up the front at night with star shells to prevent the Japanese from infiltrating the marine lines.

The major weapons of the marines were now the P-51 fighter planes dropping napalm and the tanks with flamethrowers, burning up the caves and sealing the holes. But the infantry had to go in there with the flame-throwers and grenades and make sure that the holes were really empty and were sealed. Since the Twenty-seventh Marines no longer existed, its surviving men became members of a Composite Battalion. Fewer than five hundred men were all that remained of the regiment's roster of 3,000. They continued to fight under Lieutenant Colonel Donn Robertson, the only original battalion commander of the regiment still in action.

On that day the war on Iwo Jima was declared to be over, two Medals of Honor were won. One of them went to Private George Phillips, a replacement who smothered a Japanese grenade and saved the lives of three men at the cost of his own. The other went to Private Franklin Sigler. His squad leader and assistant were shot down, and he took command of the leaderless squad and led it in battle that day. Although he was wounded, he carried three marines to safety and returned to lead the squad until ordered to go back to the aid station for treatment.

194 IWO JIMA

The day the war on Iwo ended finally came to an end, with the marines in their usual defense perimeter waiting for the usual Japanese night infiltration and the almost constant mortar and machine gun fire. Three miles south, they could see the flickering on the three divisional motion picture screens.

A marine on guard duty near Suribachi created a sensation when he fantasized into his walkie-talkie, pretending he was a newscaster announcing that the war had ended with victory in Europe. The fake message was received in the radio center of an offshore ship, where the radio operator was monitoring foreign broadcasts. He spread the news through the fleet, and pandemonium hit Iwo Jima for fifteen minutes, until the report was found to be false.

That night, General Kuribayashi learned of Admiral Nimitz's proclamation from Japan, where radio Tokyo sent special messages to the defenders of Iwo Jima, glorifying them and telling them to continue their valiant defense and kill Americans. Little children from Kuribayashi's home town sang a special song in honor of the defenders of Iwo Jima. General Kuribayashi vowed to continue the battle.

General Rockey that night ordered 10 percent of all his rear echelon men to be ready on an hour's notice to become riflemen at the front. Next morning 200 artillerymen went into the infantry line, with fifty-five amphtrac drivers and 105 truck drivers. Within two days more than half of the men were dead or wounded.

On March 17, D + 26, Admiral Nimitz did it again. He issued a special communique which declared that Iwo Jima had been officially secured and that organized Japanese resistance had ended.

General Holland Smith left Iwo Jima that day on Admiral Nimitz's personal airplane. A press conference was held at Pearl Harbor, and from that point on Iwo Jima was referred to in the past tense.

But somebody forgot to tell the Japanese of Cushman's Pocket and The Gorge. The marines still fighting began to be a little bitter about the misinformation that was reaching the

And the Fighting Went On and On   195

people at home. If the battle was over, then why were they still out there being wounded and killed?

That night, General Kuribayashi sent his last message to Tokyo. The Japanese ammunition was exhausted and the water was gone. He issued his last order to the troops:

"All surviving officers and men:

"The battle situation has come to the last moment.

"I want my surviving officers and men to go out and attack the enemy tonight.

"Each man!

Go out simultaneously at midnight and attack the enemy until the last. You have devoted yourselves to the Emperor. Don't think of yourselves.

"I am always at the head of you all."

At midnight, he told Tokyo, he would lead the final offensive.

That night, 400 men moved to a last-stand cave near Kitano Point. The next morning, a *banzai* attack was staged just before dawn. But messages continued to emanate from Kuribayashi's headquarters. On March 21, a message from the general was received on Chichi Jima, saying that the Japanese were still fighting on Iwo Jima and that the enemy line was only 200 meters from the general's command post. The marines were attacking with flamethrowers and tanks. They had advised the Japanese by leaflet to surrender, but the Japanese had only laughed.

"All officers and men of Chichi Jima. Goodbye," said the message from the general. And that was the last that was heard.

On D + 27, the Japanese in Cushman's Pocket were still fighting, but squeezed into a deep gorge about 200 yards long. The area was so small that artillery could no longer be used by the marines for fear of killing other marines. The marines brought up rocket launchers mounted on sleds, and they fired rockets at the Japanese. But the fighting went on. Bulldozers came up to make roads so that the tanks could come in and use their flamethrowers. By mid-afternoon, the Shermans were searing all the targets. By sundown, there was no more answering fire from the Japanese. Cushman's

196 IWO JIMA

Pocket was finally overrun by a combination of old hands and replacements.

That night, a series of explosions shook The Gorge, where engineers detonated 8,500 pounds of explosive in a chain of five explosions. This ended resistance in The Gorge.

In the Fourth Division sector, the last of the snipers was knocked off in the Turkey Knob area.

From this point on it was all mopping up, but more marines and more Japanese would die in this effort. Private First Class Walter Josefiak, nineteen years old, was at the point of a six-man mopping up patrol with Rusty, his war dog. The team had cleaned out two pockets of stragglers, killing seven Japanese, and were moving toward the next cave. Suddenly the dog growled. Josefiak whirled and shot a Japanese with his carbine. The dog growled again, and Josefiak shot another Japanese. Another sniper opened up. Josefiak wounded him, but was wounded in turn, and grenades began flying. Rusty went to his master's side and lay between him and the cave mouth. A grenade exploded and hit Josefiak. He yelled for someone to get the dog. Another grenade blew, and Rusty took the blast to shield his master. He died instantly. Josefiak managed to get to the safety of a boulder, and he was extricated, but he died that night at the Third Division hospital. He and the dog were both buried on Iwo Jima in the Third Division cemetery.

The Fourth Division left Iwo Jima on March 19. The Fifth Division survivors left on March 27, and the Third Division got ready to pull out. General Schmidt closed down the Fifth Amphibious Corps command and flew to Pearl Harbor. The 147th Army Regiment would finish the mopping up operations against the Japanese and take over occupation duties.

Then, on March 26 before dawn, some three hundred Japanese launched a final suicide attack. It started at 5:15 A.M. with a burst of small arms fire in a bivouac area west of the No. 2 Airfield. Here were supply troops, air force troops, Seabees, and antiaircraft gunners. These were not infantry, and the Japanese had chosen an area to inflict maximum damage. They attacked from three sides. Luckily, among the American troops were the Fifth Pioneer Battalion, marine engineers, who were first of all marines. The Japanese came slashing through the tent lines with bayonet and sword. Marine Lieutenant Harry L. Martin led the defense, and organized his troops to fight. The fighting was bloody and awful. Fifth Division infantry men standing by to go to the beach and leave the island came back to fight. Finally, three hours after the battle began, an army company appeared with a flamethrower tank. When the battle ended, forty-four airmen were dead, eighty-eight were wounded. Nine marines were killed and thirty-one were wounded. More than 260 Japanese bodies were found, and eighteen prisoners were taken.

This was truly the end of the fighting on Iwo Jima. And when it was over, the marines had suffered 25,851 casualties on this island. It was the costliest battle in which the United States Marines had ever fought. In that last action, the marines had won their final Medal of Honor on Iwo Jima. It went to Lieutenant Martin for his organization of the defense and his valiant personal conduct that resulted in his death.

And so the saga of Iwo Jima came to an end.

The last word was said by one of the marines as he stood at the rail of his transport and looked out over the gray desolate rock.

"Iwo Jima! God damn the place. We won. But I wouldn't come here again for all the money in the world."

NOTES

1 The American Plan

The difficulties between the United States and Japan date back to the Treaty of Portsmouth of 1905. Theodore Roosevelt at that time prevented the Japanese military from securing a large cash payment from the Russians, who had lost the Russo-Japanese War. In equity that was only proper, since the Japanese had started the war with the unprovoked attack on the Russian fleet at Port Arthur. But the Japanese military men did not look at it that way, and they were counting on the cash to finance military expansion. Instead they had to look forward to a long period of lean years, punctuated by the first World War and the long occupation of Siberia. But as of 1905, America became Japan's declared natural enemy, and the Japanese naval war plan was drawn with the U.S. as the adversary.

The Americans responded in kind, and Plan Orange supposed the Japanese to be the American enemy. From there things went from bad to worse over a period of thirty-five years, as the Japanese military sought and finally achieved control of the government, having wrested it from the hands of the civil political leaders. They were able to do this because of the nature of the Meiji Constitution that gave the military special powers. The Japanese constitution of 1947 was drawn carefully to avoid such a thing's happening again.

Several matters concerning the war in the beginning merit consideration beyond the parameters of this book. One is to speculate a little as to what would have happened in the Pacific War if President Roosevelt had not allowed himself to be persuaded in December 1941 to throw the whole weight of the American nation against Hitler and instead had done what most American military and civil leaders wanted, to concentrate on the war against Japan, which had attacked the United States. Certainly, General MacArthur would then have been reinforced in the Philippines, and if that had been done there is a very good chance that he would have defeated the Japanese and saved the islands. The Japanese were greatly overextended in the Pacific at the time, and they were losing the battle of Bataan. But in the absence of aid from America, our troops were victims of hunger and disease much more than of the Japanese.

Quite probably if the war had been prosecuted against the Japanese wholeheartedly from the beginning, it would have ended in 1943 after the defeat of the Japanese in the South Pacific, and the atomic bomb would never have been employed. This first chapter of the book depends on much that I have studied before for preparation of other volumes of this series and for such books as *Japan's War*.

2 The American Assault Force

The major source for the chapter was the Cincpac records, but I also relied heavily on the Dyer[1] book, and my own *Nimitz and His Admirals*, published by Weybright and Talley in 1968.

3 The Defenses of Iwo Jima

For this chapter I relied on the Japanese records and their official war history and the Ross[2] book about Iwo Jima.

4 Softening Up for Iwo Jima

The story of Task Force 58 comes from the CincPac records and *Nimitz and His Admirals*, the diary of Admiral Matome Ugaki, and the Fane[3] book about Underwater Demolition Teams and the navy records on that subject.

---

[1] see Bibliography, page
[2] see Bibliography, page 205
[3] see Bibliography, page 204

5 The Landings

This chapter relied heavily on Samuel Eliot Morison's book on the last days of the Pacific War, Volume 14 of his *History of U.S. Naval Operations in World War II*[4]. I also used the Ross[5] book, the three marine divisional histories, and Stanley[6] Smith's book of excerpted writings of marines and correspondents.

6 Crossing the Island

The story of the crossing of the island by the Twenty-eighth Marines comes largely from the Smith[7] account, written by marine correspondent Wheeler. Some of it comes from Ross[8], and some from Wheeler's own book, *Iwo*[9].

7 The Airfield

The tales of the marines fighting their way across and up the island are from the three marine histories, Stanley Smith[10], and Ross[11], for the most part.

8 The Twenty-Fifth Marines Had a Little Problem . . .

The story of Sergeant Gallant's adventures is from material in his own account, written as a combat correspondent, as it appeared in the Stanley Smith[12] book.

9 "The Most Savage and the Most Costly Battle"

The material about the situation on the beaches is mostly from Morison[13] and from the three marine divisional histories.

---

[4] see Bibliography, page 204
[5] see Bibliography, page 205
[6] see Bibliography, page 205
[7] see Bibliography, page 205
[8] see Bibliography, page 205
[9] see Bibliography, page 205
[10] see Bibliography, page 205
[11] see Bibliography, page 205
[12] see Bibliography, page 205
[13] see Bibliography, page 204

10 Night

The story of the marines on Suribachi and its shoulders is from the Fifth Marine Division's history and from Stanley Smith[14], with some material from Ross[15], particularly about the Japanese naval reconnaissance of the beach.

11 The Second Phase

This chapter depended on the Fourth and Fifth Division histories, and the Smith[16] book for the story of Lieutenant Bates. The material about the beaches and the naval bombardment is from [17]Morison.

12 The Most Dangerous Game

This chapter came from the divisional histories, and from Morison[18] and Ross[19]. The stories about Lieutenant Wells and Easy Company are from the Smith[20] book, and the story of the *kamikaze* attack is from material gathered for my book, *The Kamikazes*, and the Ugaki diary.

13 The Capture of Mt. Suribachi

This story of Suribachi is from the Smith[21] book and the Fifth Division history, and the material about the navy from Morison[22].

14 The Medics

The material about the medics is from the three divisional histories and from Ross[23].

---

[14]see Bibliography, page 205
[15]see Bibliography, page 205
[16]see Bibliography, page 205
[17]see Bibliography, page 204
[18]see Bibliography, page 204
[19]see Bibliography, page 205
[20]see Bibliography, page 205
[21]see Bibliography, page 205
[22]see Bibliography, page 204
[23]see Bibliography, page 205

15 The Main Attack
The stories in this chapter come from Ross[24] and the Boei[25] history, and the Fourth and Third Marine Division histories.

16 And in the Second Week . . .
The sources here include the Fourth Division history. Ross[26], the Boei[27] history.

17 The Meatgrinder
The material on the Meatgrinder is from the Fourth Division history and Ross[28]. The material on the anti-Nimitz campaign in the American press is from Ross[29].

18 Attrition
The three divisional histories were the basic source for the chapter, plus material from Smith[30] and Ross[31].

19 But a Limited Success
Morison[32] was the source for much material in this chapter, and also the three marine divisional histories.

20 A Little Help
The three divisional histories were the source, plus Smith[33] and Ross[34].

21 Pressure
I consulted Wheeler[35], Ross[36], Smith[37] and the divisional histories for the stories here.

---

[24] see Bibliography, page 205
[25] see Bibliography, page 204
[26] see Bibliography, page 205
[27] see Bibliography, page 204
[28] see Bibliography, page 205
[29] see Bibliography, page 205
[30] see Bibliography, page 205
[31] see Bibliography, page 205
[32] see Bibliography, page 204
[33] see Bibliography, page 205
[34] see Bibliography, page 205
[35] see Bibliography, page 205
[36] see Bibliography, page 205
[37] see Bibliography, page 205

22 The Waste of the Azusa Unit

The Divine Wind[38], the Ugaki diary[39], and Morison[40] were the sources for this material on the Azusa raid on Ulithi— Morison because he never mentioned it, which means that most of the naval people in Ulithi were completely unaware of the Japanese attack.

23 And the Fighting Went On and On

This chapter depended on the divisional histories and on the Ross[41] book.

---

[38] see Bibliography, page 204
[39] see Bibliography, page 205
[40] see Bibliography, page 204
[41] see Bibliography, page 205

BIBLIOGRAPHY

Arthur, Robert A. and Kenneth Cohlmia. *The Third Marine Division*, Washington: Infantry Journal Press, 1948.

Bartley, Whitman S. *Iwo Jima, Ambitious Epic*. Washington: Historical Division, U.S. Marine Corps, 1954.

Boei Senshi Shitsu, Iwo Jima Sakusen. (Japanese Defense Agency War History room, volume on Japanese Army Operations on Iwo Jima. Part of the *Official Japanese History of the Pacific War*. Tokyo: Japanese Defense Agency Press, 1975.

Chapin, John C. *The Fifth Marine Division in World War II*. Washington: Historical Branch, U.S. Marine Corps, 1945.

Dyer, George C. *The Amphibions Come to Conquer*. Washington: U.S. Navy, 1958.

Fane, Francis Douglas and Don Moore. *The Naked Warriors*. New York: Appleton-Century-Crofts, 1956.

Garand, George W. and Truman R. Strobridge. *History of U.S. Marine Corps Operations in World War II*, volume 4. *Western Pacific Operations*, Washington: Historical Division, U.S. Marine Corps, 1971.

Hoyt, Edwin P. *The Last Kamikaze, Admiral Matome Ugaki* and *The Fall of the Japanese Navy*. New York: Praeger, 1992.

Inoguchi, Rikihei and Tadashi Nakajima, with Roger Pineau. *The Divine Wind*. New York: Bantam Books, 1958.

Morison, Samuel Eliot. *History of United States Naval Operations in World War II*, volume 14. *Victory in the Pacific, 1945*, Boston: Atlantic Little Brown, 1975.

Newcomb, Richard F. *Iwo Jima*. New York: Holt Rinehart and Winston, 1965.

Proehl, Carl W., ed. *The Fourth Marine Division in World*

War II, narrative by David Dempsey. Washington: Infantry Journal Press, 1946.

Ross, Bill D. *Iwo Jima, Legacy of Valor*. New York: Vanguard Press, 1985.

Smith, Holland M. and Percy Finch. *Coral and Brass*. New York: Charles Scribner's Sons, 1949.

Smith, Stanley E. *The United States Marine Corps in World War II*, New York: Random House, 1969.

Wheeler, Richard, *Iwo*. New York: Lippincott & Crowell, 1980.

INDEX

Adamson, William, 120
Aid station on Iwo Jima, 110–112
Airfield No. 1, 15, 47–54, 65, 78, 81, 83, 118, 121, 166; capture by U. S. troops, 81
Airfield No. 2, 15, 121, 173
Air raid, 11–12, 17, 22
Air superiority: Japan, 4; United States, 4
Aleutian Islands, 4
Anderson, Carl E., 82
Antonelli, John, 186
Anzio, 129
Archambault, Raoul J., 116
Arkansas, 23
Arnold, Henry H., 4, 9–10, 185; recommendation to seize Iwo Jima, 10
Athene, 68
Atsuchi, Kanehiko, 31, 99, 103, 104
Auburn, 149, 157
Awatsu, Captain, 124
Azusa Unit (Japan), 188–190

B–17 aircraft, 2
B–24 aircraft, 12, 17, 24, 56
B–25 aircraft, 4
B–29 Superfortresses, 5, 7–8, 9–10, 11, 12, 19, 56 157, 160, 185–186
Banzai attacks, 70, 72, 91, 94, 95, 99, 103, 114, 184, 195
Basilione, John, 48
Bates, Wesley, 32, 39–40, 80
Beary, Donald B., 11
Benedict, Harold, 108
Berry, Charles J., 153; Medal of Honor awarded to, 153
Bismarck Sea, 98, 99
Black Widow night fighters, 166
Blandy, William, H. P., 10, 23–24
Blessman, 26
Block, G., 108
Bombardment, 20–27
Bonin Islands, 10, 13; Chichi Jima, 13, 14
Bradley, John, 108

208 Index

Bunker Hill, 21
Butler, John, 161

Caddy, William, 152–153; Medal of Honor awarded to, 153
Callahan, Donald, 142
Carrier superiority: Japan, 3; United States, 3
Carter, Andrew, 151
Casualties: American 33, 34, 48–49, 55–57, 67, 68, 91, 100, 102, 108, 117, 119, 121, 121, 126, 128, 131, 134, 135, 140, 148, 150, 154, 165, 172, 183–184, 187, 192, 197; Japanese, 40, 43, 44, 48, 79, 91, 108–109, 112, 150, 184, 197
Catalina flying boats, 157
Cates, Clifton B., 10, 141, 143, 144, 145, 146, 155, 182, 191; predicting fall of the Meatgrinder, 155–156
Chamberlain, Reid Carlos, 175–176; Army Distinguished Service Medal awarded to, 175; death of, 176
Chaney, James, 129, 192
Chester, 23
Chicago Tribune, 1399
China, 6
Churchill, Winston, 1, 192
Cobia, 14
Cole, Darrell, 52
Columbia Victory, 126
Combined Fleet (Japan), 22, 26
Connally, Paul, 183

Corral Sea, battle of, 3
Cowpens, 21
Crecink, William, 154

Defenses of Iwo Jima, 13–19
Devoe, Frank, 53, 54
Dinah Might Superfortress, 156–157, 158
Dollings, Ray, 50
Doolittle, James, 4
Doolittle raid, 4
Duplantis, Wendell, 115
Durgin, C. T., 23
Duryea, Justin, 186
Dutch East Indies, 3

Eighth Marines (U.S.), 124
801st Air Group (Japan), 27
Eldorado, 33, 70, 139, 185
Enterprise, 185
Erskine, Graves B.,: release of Third Marine Regiment, requesting, 149; Third Marine Division cemetery, dedicating, 193
Essex, 21
Eutsey, A1, 134
Evans, Holly, 120

Faulkner, Bill, 34–35
Fertig, Wendell, 175
Fifth Air Fleet (Japan), 19, 22
Fifth Amphibious Corps (U.S.), 28–29, 163–164
Fifth Marine Division (U.S.), 83, 85, 92, 93, 117, 119, 122, 131, 133, 146, 151, 152, 164, 179–180, 186,

187, 196, 197; casualties, 121, 134, 150, 187
Fifth Pioneer Battalion (U.S.), 196–197
Fifth Reconnaissance Company (U.S.), 128
Fifth Tank Battalion (U.S.), 78
509th Anti-Aircraft Battalion (U.S.), 124
Forrestal, James V., 109, 139–140; public reply to letter voicing concern, 139–140
Fourth Marine Division (U.S.), 65, 68, 78, 83, 92, 113, 117–118, 119, 121, 127, 130, 134, 141, 165, 178, 179, 187, 196; casualties, 117, 128, 135, 148, 150
Fourteenth Marine Division (U.S.), 85

Gagnon, Rent, 108
Gallant, T. Gardy, 55–60, 63–64
Gamble, 26
Germany, 140
Ginga bombers, 188–189
Good, Roscoe, 79
Grossi, Dominic, 116
Guadalcanal, 4, 140
Guam, 191

Hale, Willis H., 11
Halsey, William F., 5, 6
Hancock, 21
Hanson, Henry, 107
Harmon, Millard F., 11

Harrell, William 151–152; Medal of Honor awarded to, 151
Hart, Brigadier General, 29
Hawkins, Keith, 134
Hayes, Ira, 108
Heinze, Rodney, 116
Henry A. Wiley, 91
Hermle, Leo, 29; 68
Hill, Harry W., 10, 185, 192
History of U.S. Naval Operations in World Warr II Morison, 190
Hitler, Adolf, 2
Holder, William, 100, 101, 102
Hong Kong, 2

Ichimaru, Toshinosuke, 13, 132, 184; Toyoda's message of encouragement to, 132; vowing to defend Iwo Jima to death, 114
Idaho, 23, 115
Ikeda, Colonel, 113
India, 6
Inouye, Samaji, 114

Jacobson, Douglas T., 122, 142–143
Japan: animosity toward U.S., 1; carrier superiority, 3; defense of Iwo Jima, 13–19; defense perimeter, 4–5; Doolittle raid on, 4; Expansionism, 2–3; Hong Kong, capture of, 2; Imperial General Headquarters, 6, 28, 22; newspapers in

Japan speculating attack on, 96; Okinawa, U.S. plans for attack on, 91, 200, 118, 124, 140, 160, 185; Operation Tan, 23, 27, 188; Pear Harbor, attack on, 1, 2; Radio Tokyo, 138, 194; Russo-Japanese War, 1; Sho I operation, 55; Singapore, capture of, 2–3, suicide air warfare, tactic of, 19–20; Tokyo, bombing of, 187

Johnson, Chandler, 35, 79, 83, 96, 100, 103, 104, 150; American flag raising on Mt. Suribachi, 103, 107–108; attack plan, 103

Josefiak, Walter, 196

Josephy, Alvin, 170, 171, 172, 174, 176

Julian, Joseph, 186–187; death of, 187; Medal of Honor awarded to, 187

Kalen, John, 52

Kamikaze attacks, 7, 19, 20, 23, 97–99, 128, 140, 188

Kato, Kunimatsu, 128

Kearns, Raphael, 67

Keller, Harold, 106

Keokuk, 99

Kimmel, Husband E., 160

King, Ernest J., 3–4

Kinkaid, Thomas, 23

Kurelik, Edward, 71, 73–74, 77

Kuibayaski, Tadamichi, 13–14, 15–16, 17–18, 35, 44, 50, 69, 75–76, 77, 94, 114, 133, 138, 145, 145, 148, 163, 192, 194; concealing dead Japanese soldiers, giving orders for, 112; defense plan, 16; final offensive, leading, 195; refusing to grant permission for staging *banzi* attack, 99, 103; reports to Tokyo, 69, 76, 96, 143, 195; *samurai* spirit, instilling in his men, 17

LaBelle, James 182

Landing Craft Inventory (LCI) gunboats, 25

Landings on Iwo Jima, 28–38

Lanigan, John, 31, 50, 66, 78, 144

Lardner, John, 48

Leader, Robert, 106

Leahy, William D., 4

Leims, John, 168–169; Medal of Honor awarded to, 169

LeMay, Curtis, 7, 185

Leutze, 25

Lexington, 3, 21

Lindberg, Charles, 107

Liversedge, Harry, 31, 82, 103

Lowery, Louis, 105, 107

Lucas, Jim, 142

Lummus, Jack, 181–182; death of, 182; Medal of Honor awarded to, 182

Lunga Point, 98

MacArthur, Douglas, 2, 5–6, 10, 139, 140

Index 211

Main line of American attack, 113–138
Mannert L. Abele, 83
Mariana Islands, 4–5, 6, 9–11; fall of, 5
Mariedas, James, 37
Marshall, George C., 4, 9
Marshall Islands, 4
Martin, Harry L., 197
Mears, Dwayne, 40, 134
Meatgrinder, The (Japanese defense system), 119, 121, 122, 136, 139–148, 150, 154, 155–156, 158, 161, 182, 187; major assault on, 141–142; weak spot in, attempts to find, 145
Michaelis, James, 107
Midway operation, 4
Mitscher, Marc A., 10
Montgomery, Bernard Law, 6
Morison, Samuel Eliot, 190
Mt. Suribachi, 15, 31, 78, 79, 83, 93, 95, 100, 113–114, 117, 136–137, 166–167, 192; air attacks on, 78, 79; American flag raising on, 103, 106–109; capture of, 103–109
Mowrey, Hap, 79–80
Mulvey, William, 164, 165
Mustain, Hollis, 52

Nevada, 23, 25
New Guinea, 3
New York, 23
New York Daily News, 1399

Nimitz, Chester W., 6, 11–12, 139, 191, 194; declaring victory on Iwo Jima, 191–192; ordering Iwo Jima be given top priority for bombardment, 12
Ninth Marines (U.S.), 118, 119, 120, 124, 127, 150, 173
Nishi, Takeichi, 14, 18, 130, 136
Nisshu Maru, 14

Ohnishi, Takejiro, 7
Okinawa, U.S. plans for attack on, 92, 100, 118, 124, 140, 160, 185
O'Mealia, Robert, 154
109th Infantry Division (Japan), 13, 17
Operation Tan (Japan), 23, 27, 188

Palau Islands, 4
PBM flying boats, 129
Pearce, Thomas, 150
Pearl Harbor, attack on, 1, 2, 160
Pensacola, 23, 24–25, 115; attack on, 23
P–51 fighter planes, 8, 10, 166, 192, 193
Philippines, 2, 5, 6, 7, 97; Leyte, invasion of, 7; Mindanao, 6–7
Phillips, George, 193
Plan Orange (U.S.), 1
Pollock, Edwin, 145

Rabaul, 3
Reich, Dick, 154
Rice, Harold, 34
Ridlon, Walter, 135, 154
Roach, Phil, 34
Robertson, Donn, 193
Robeson, James, 106, 107
Rockey, Keller E., 10, 68, 153, 191, 194
Rockmore, Clayton, 116
Roosevelt, Franklin D., 2, 6, 192
Roosevelt, Theodore, 1
Roselle, Jr., Benjamin, 36
Rosenthal, Joe, 108
Rozek, Leo, 106
Ruhl, Don, 94
Russo-Japanese War, 1

Salgo, Oscar, 166
Salt Lake City, 23, 185, 193
Samoa, 4
San Jacinto, 21
Saratoga, 97–98; attack on, 98
Savage, Merritt, 40
Schmidt, Harry, 10, 119, 140, 149, 159, 161, 166, 180, 191, 196
Schrier, Harold, 103, 106, 107, 108
Scout-Sniper Platoon (U.S.), 92, 100–101
Second Armored Amphibious Battalion (U.S.), 30
Second Mixed Brigade (Japan), 128
Senda, Sadasue, 119; defense system of, 119
Seventh Army Air Force (U.S.), 1, 16–17; ordered to keep Iwo Jima neutralized, 12, 166
Shaker, Conrad, 34–35
Sherman, Forrest, 10
Sherrod, Robert, 55, 111
Sho I operation (Japan), 5, 7
Shokaku, 3
Sigler, Franklin, 193
Singapore, 2
601st Air Group (Japan), 27
Smith, Holland M. ("Howling Mad"), 10, 28, 65, 70, 77, 92, 109, 118, 129–130, 131, 149, 158, 159, 160, 161–162, 191, 194; refusing request for reserves, 131; statements on fall of Iwo Jima, 129–130
Snyder, Howard, 41, 74, 106, 107
Sousley, Franklin, 108
Spruance, Raymond, 10
Stalin, Joseph, 192
Stein, Tony, 40, 133, 150
Stephenson, Edward, 130
Strand, Mike, 108
Suter, Father, 109

Tabert, Frederick, 40
Task Force 38 (U.S.), 5
Task Force 58 (U.S.), 10, 20, 100
Tatsumi, Major, 48
Tennessee, 23
Teraoka, Kimpei, 19
Terry, 133

Texas, 23
Third Air Fleet (Japan), 19, 21–22
Third Fleet (U.S), 5
Third Marine Division (U.S.), 29, 78, 99, 199, 120, 122, 127, 130, 140, 149, 150, 154, 158, 179, 187; casulaties, 183–184; Erskine dedicating Third Marine Division cemetery, 193
Third Tank Battalion (U.S.), 120
Thirteenth Marines (U.S.), 79
Thomas, Ernest, 95, 106, 107
Thomas E. Fraser, 83
Thostensen, Thorburn, 32, 35
309th Independent Infantry Battalion (Japan), 124
311th Independent Infantry Battalion (Japan), 48
312th Independent Infantry Battalion (Japan), 43
Tokyo, bombing of, 187
Tokyo Rose, 138
Toyoda, Soemu, 132, 188
Treadway, James, 32–33
Turner, Richmond Kelly, 10, 28, 30, 52, 53, 92, 149, 160, 161, 165, 185, 191
Tuscaloosa, 23, 185, 193
Twentieth Air Force (U.S.), 10, 118, 185
Twenty-first Marines (U.S.), 99, 199, 130, 141, 150, 164, 173
Twenty-third Infantry (U.S.), 68

Twenty-third Marines (U.S.), 51, 65, 75, 78, 124, 127, 142, 143–144, 164
Twenty-fourth Marines (U.S.), 68, 84, 119, 135, 145, 164, 165
Twenty-fifth Marines (U.S.), 38, 55–65, 68, 78, 81–82, 124, 131, 144, 145, 146
Twenty-sixth Marines (U.S.), 78, 80, 117, 122, 178; casualties, 154
Twenty-seventh Marines (U.S.), 65, 78, 80, 128, 131, 164, 186; casualties, 192; surviving men of Marines becoming members of Composite Battalion, 193
Twenty-eighth Marines (U.S.), 35, 40, 65, 70, 73, 78, 79, 82–83, 100, 133, 150, 1161, 178; capture of Mt. Suribachi, 103–109

Ugaki, Matome, 19, 22–23, 26–27, 189
United States, 3; army and navy dispute over approach to Japan, 6; censorship of press, 140; Iwo Jima as U.S. territory, 192; Joint Chiefs of Staff, 5; land-based aircraft used in support of operations, 11; navy and army dispute over approach to Japan, 6; newspapers criticizing American leadership in the Pacific,

214 Index

139; Pacific war plan, 1–8; Plan Orange, 1
U.S. Fleet, 1, 5

Valbracht, Louis, 48–49
Vandegrift, General, 175
Vicksburg, 23

Wagner, LaVerne, 37
Wahlen, George, 152; Medal of Honor awarded to, 152
Wake Island, 23
Waller, Jr., Harcourt E., 123
Washington, 81, 86
Washington Times Herald, 1399
Watson, Wilson D., 127
Weaver, Charles, 134
Wells, Greeley, 41–43, 44–46, 70, 72, 73, 83, 93, 95
Wensinger, Walter, 31, 47, 50, 78
Wheeler, Richard, 41, 70, 72, 73–74
Wilkins, Aaron G., 40, 133–134
Williams, Jack, 152; Medal of Honor awarded to, 152
Wilson, Robert, 134
Wood, Alan, 107
Wornham, Thomas, 31, 47, 49, 192
Worsham, William, 52, 54
Wright, Frank, 34, 39

Yamamoto, Isoroku, 3, 4; Midway operation, insistence on, 4

Zimmerman, Arthur, 53–54
Zuck, Leo, 39
Zuikaku, 3
Zurlinden, Cyril, 75

WORLD WAR II HISTORIES
by Edwin P. Hoyt

WAR IN THE PACIFIC

TRIUMPH OF JAPAN	75792-3/$4.50 US/$5.50 Can
STIRRINGS	75793-1/$3.95 US/$4.95 Can
SOUTH PACIFIC	76158-0/$4.50 US/$5.50 Can
THE JUNGLES OF NEW GUINEA	
	75750-8/$4.95 US/$5.95 Can
ALEUTIANS	76316-8/$4.99 US/$5.99 Can
MACARTHUR'S RETURN	76165-3/$4.99 US/$5.99 Can

WAR IN EUROPE

BLITZKRIEG	76155-6/$4.99 US/$5.99 Can
THE FALL OF FRANCE	76156-4/$4.99 US/$5.99 Can
THE BATTLE OF BRITAIN	
	76482-2/$4.50 US/$5.50 Can
BATTLES IN THE BALKANS	
	76483-0/$4.99 US/$5.99 Can

Buy these books at your local bookstore or use this coupon for ordering:

Mail to: Avon Books, Dept BP, Box 767, Rte 2, Dresden, TN 38225   B
Please send me the book(s) I have checked above.
☐ My check or money order—no cash or CODs please—for $_____ is enclosed (please add $1.50 to cover postage and handling for each book ordered—Canadian residents add 7% GST).
☐ Charge my VISA/MC Acct#_____ Exp Date_____
Phone No _____ Minimum credit card order is $6.00 (please add postage and handling charge of $2.00 plus 50 cents per title after the first two books to a maximum of six dollars—Canadian residents add 7% GST). For faster service, call 1-800-762-0779. Residents of Tennessee, please call 1-800-633-1607. Prices and numbers are subject to change without notice. Please allow six to eight weeks for delivery.

Name_____

Address_____

City_____ State/Zip_____

HOY 0992

#1
HIS THIRD CONSECUTIVE NUMBER ONE BESTSELLER!

James Clavell's
WHIRLWIND

70312-2/$6.99 US/$7.99 CAN

From the author of *Shōgun* and *Noble House*—
the newest epic in the magnificent Asian Saga
is now in paperback!

"WHIRLWIND IS A CLASSIC—FOR OUR TIME!"
Chicago Sun-Times

WHIRLWIND

is the gripping epic of a world-shattering upheaval that alters the destiny of nations. Men and women barter for their very lives. Lovers struggle against heartbreaking odds. And an ancient land battles to survive as a new reign of terror closes in...

Buy these books at your local bookstore or use this coupon for ordering:

Mail to: Avon Books, Dept BP, Box 767, Rte 2, Dresden, TN 38225   B
Please send me the book(s) I have checked above.
☐ My check or money order—no cash or CODs please—for $_____ is enclosed (please add $1.50 to cover postage and handling for each book ordered—Canadian residents add 7% GST).
☐ Charge my VISA/MC Acct# _____ Exp Date _____
Phone No _____ Minimum credit card order is $6.00 (please add postage and handling charge of $2.00 plus 50 cents per title after the first two books to a maximum of six dollars—Canadian residents add 7% GST). For faster service, call 1-800-762-0779. Residents of Tennessee, please call 1-800-633-1607. Prices and numbers are subject to change without notice. Please allow six to eight weeks for delivery.

Name _____
Address _____
City _____ State/Zip _____

JCW 0892